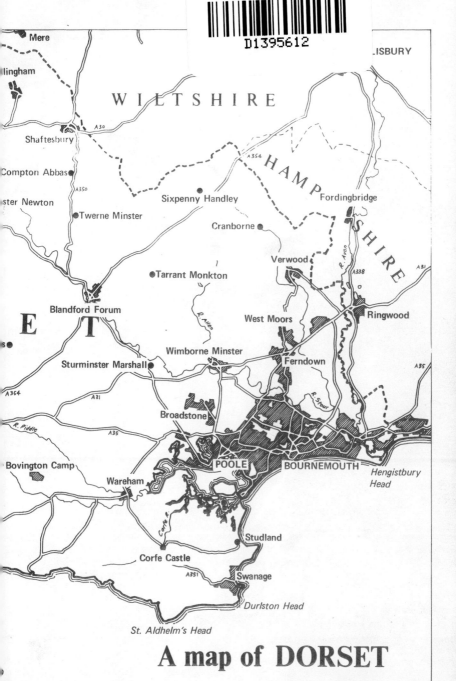

A map of DORSET

History, People
and Places in
Dorset

Forde Abbey

History, People and Places in

DORSET

by Garry Hogg

SPURBOOKS LIMITED

Published by Spurbooks Limited
6 Parade Court, Bourne End, Buckinghamshire

ISBN 0 904978 03 6

Designed and Produced by
Mechanick Exercises, London

Typesetting by Inforum Limited, Portsmouth
Printed in Great Britain by Chapel River Press, Andover

FOR MIKE AND ANNE

Contents

Illustrations

1. Introduction

IF I COULD CHOOSE among the forty-odd English counties the one in which I should be most content to live out the remainder of my life, to be buried and have the still living turf folded over my grave, it would without question be Dorset.

I knew the county first when, as a schoolboy, I used to cycle from my Hertfordshire home to join my family at their habitual seaside resort on the Cornish coast. The moment I passed out of the New Forest near Ringwood I knew that I was on the threshold of the West Country; Dorset was its magic gateway. In my mid-teens I would stop off at some farm on the Dorset-Somerset border and work in the harvest fields for a week or two, exchanging the meagre World War One rationing for the good fare still to be found in this essentially agricultural region. To this day I can recall my astonishment when, being accompanied by a school friend on this 300-mile cycle-trip, he looked askance and declined the fare so lavishly spread out on the well scrubbed kitchen table of a farm where we had offered our services—notably the clotted cream that was, for me, its most luscious ingredient. Does he now, a Professor of Economy at Oxbridge, remember those distant days and the readiness with which I added his portion to my own?

Later, condemned by circumstances to live in the North Midlands, I took every opportunity I could to turn south-by-west and revive my memories of Dorset. I have long lost count of the number of times I have passed through or, even better, lingered in that beloved county; nor is the tally complete, or likely to remain so, while I continue to be mobile. I have walked and cycled and more recently driven along its innumerable minor roads and twisting lanes. I have climbed to the rounded summits of the turf-clad hills on which Iron Age Man and others laid out their hill-fort ramparts of turf and ditch: Bulbarrow and Eggardon, Rawlsbury and Hambledon, Badbury, Hod Hill, and many others. I have lazed in the wide valleys of the Stour and Piddle and Frome and their tributaries, in the dairy-farming regions of north-east Dorset. For yet another distant view across these incomparable rolling

Rolling Landscape

downs I have climbed to the summit of Giant Hill, immediately to the north of Cerne Abbas, and sat on the forehead of the Cerne Giant himself, monarch of all I surveyed.

It is probably true that I did not begin to appreciate to the full the subtle magic of Dorset until I became engrossed in the novels of Thomas Hardy—the 'Wessex' novels. In this county he was born, lived, and died; in the little church at Stinsford a mile or two south of Dorchester (his 'Casterbridge') his heart is buried, though his ashes lie in Westminster Abbey. The essence of Dorset is 'Hardy Country', to an even greater extent than Warwickshire is 'Shakespeare Country'; the county is as essential a 'character' in his novels as any of their men and women. His 'Egdon Heath' to the north-west of Wareham is every bit as much a character in his masterpiece, *The Return of the Native*, as Damon Wildeve and Diggory Venn the 'reddleman' who diced by the light of thirteen glowworms, having met there at midnight. Much of this heathland has long been used by the Ministry of Defence, but sections of it are, under pressure from conservationists, happily being to some extent at any rate, released for public use today; cliff-top and other tracks are being

14

Country Lane

opened as semi-rights-of-way; a concession for which all of us must be grateful until, with luck, the army moves out altogether, with all its weaponry and other 'hardware'.

Hardy did not 'make' Dorset; but he understood its peculiar magic, interpreting and communicating it for all to appreciate. You must, however, have lived in the county, not merely passed through it a hundred times, to know it to the full. He took its towns and villages, hamlets and minor landmarks, and gave them names that had a Dorset flavour, and indeed *could* have been pure Dorset; the disguise was often very thin indeed—perhaps deliberately so—and we shall come to them, one by one, in the course of the pages that follow.

The india-paper edition of each of his Wessex novels contains a map, and it is not difficult to identify the place-names that are crowded upon it, at least so far as the major items are concerned. The devotee can spend rewarding days, even weeks, tracing the identity of the less-well-known ones. Many years ago I encountered a Hardy enthusiast doing just that. I was cycling westwards, Cornwall-bound; he was walking (the only way to 'do' the Hardy Country), large-scale Ordnance Survey

15

map in hand; his rucksack bulged with the complete set of novels — the india-paper edition, luckily for him! Not until he had pinpointed the last and least important Hardy landmark would he be content to make for home. As a youth who had only just begun to read those novels, I was deeply impressed, and remain so still.

*

A county is given its shape by some act of administration, which may date back many centuries; its boundary is established, and remains constant. Indeed, the great majority of English counties retained their present outlines for centuries until, as recently as April, 1974, local government officialdom, for reasons best known to itself and certainly by no means always readily accepted by everyone involved, took bits-and-pieces from one county and incorporated them into an adjacent one. Tyne & Wear suddenly intruded between Northumberland and Durham; a chunk of the long-established North Riding of Yorkshire suddenly became Cleveland; the minuscule county of Rutland vanished completely overnight, absorbed by neighbouring Leicestershire, sunk without trace; the County of Avon as mysteriously appeared between

Hardy's 'Egdon Heath'

Gloucestershire and Somerset. There were other twists and turns of fortune, deeply resented by those who were despoiled and not necessarily relished by those upon whom the new terrain was thrust. Dorset is odd man out in this respect. Since April, 1974, the whole of Bournemouth and, as a bonus, Christchurch too, have been re-allocated and, technically at any rate, are no longer in Hampshire. The topographical writer today has to be very careful over his map references!

Dorset consists of a stretch of coastline extending from just beyond Christchurch, in the east, to a few furlongs beyond Lyme Regis to the west, some eighty miles in all. Its western border runs inland for a few miles alongside Devon, then serpentines northwards and eastwards alongside Somerset, missing Yeovil by a matter of yards, and then loops about Sherborne and Shaftesbury, with Wiltshire to the north-east, finally sloping south-eastwards against the Hampshire border, skirting Ringwood and reaching the English Channel just beyond Christchurch. At its most northerly point, close to Mere just over the Wiltshire border, you are not thirty miles from the coast; the area of the county falls short of a thousand square miles, placing it in roughly the same size category as, say, Warwickshire; it is hardly more than half the size of neighbouring Somerset, and only two-thirds the size of Hampshire even with its accretion of all Bournemouth and Christchurch.

But was is size? Or, for that matter, the lay-out of boundaries? These are purely arbitrary matters, and can be varied at authorities' whim. What *makes* a county is the skeleton that lies beneath the covering that is there for all to see; and that skeleton, and what overlies it, will have made the people who live there and will have gone some way to changing the course of history.

Though the suffix '-shire' is very rarely used, Dorset was recognised as a *schire* as long ago as 940 A.D. It has always puzzled those of us who know and love the county that the name is said to derive from the West Saxon *dorn-gweir-saete* — 'home-place of the fist-players'. Why 'fist-players', for heaven's sake? In a county of generally rounded contours, mellow stone buildings, gently-flowing streams, dairy-farm pasture-land, cosy farmhouses and thatched cottages, the implication of clenched fists, even in play, is hard to accept. The *saete* element is pure Norse, anyway: in Norway every valley farm has its hillside *saeter* where, during the milder period of the year, sheep and cattle may be based for pasture. The term would be more immediately recognisable in our north-eastern counties and in eastern Scotland, where the Scandinavian influence was always strongest.

Reference was made just now to history being changed. It is probably true to say that on the whole, history has passed Dorset lightly by, at least when compared with what has taken place in most other counties. It is true that the Duke of Monmouth landed at Lyme Regis in 1685, hell-bent on the destruction of the 'Popish Sovereign with the Blood-stained Hands', James II. But such battles as he fought did not take place on the soil of Dorset; it was in neighbouring Somerset that such 'fist-play' as he and his followers and their enemies indulged in took place. When routed, it is true that he tried to flee back the way he had come, but it was on the block at the Tower of London that he met his end.

More than sixteen centuries earlier, the Romans were moving inexorably west-wards from their beach-heads in Kent and elsewhere; it was the second Augustine Legion, commanded by Emporor Vespasian, that penetrated into Dorset and proceeded to fan out over Wessex generally. The Britons who had established the hill-forts and, most notably, built and occupied Maiden Castle, were without undue difficulty ousted from their strongholds and in due course the Roman city of Durnovaria (today's Dorchester) came into being. This was in or around the year 50 A.D. and was an event which could reasonably be described as the transition-moment from prehistory into historical record.

Castles, as the term is ordinarily understood, built of stone to withstand siege, are few and far between in this county. Corfe village, in the oddly-named Isle of Purbeck, inland from the popular little resort of Swanage, is dominated by the shell of what was built as a Norman castle by Edward I, only to be virtually destroyed by the Roundheads during the Civil War. The 'castle' that you might expect to find on account of the '-castra' in Dorchester is in fact barely a hundred years old, the headquarters and official military museum of the Dorsetshires. It is in fact prehistory, rather than history, for which Dorset is most memorable. But this is the aspect of the county which, illogically perhaps, we shall come to last.

2. The Dorset Coastline

CATEGORICAL STATEMENTS can be suspect; nevertheless it is safe to state that there is no stretch of coastline in all Britain which, for its modest length, contains a greater variety of interest than that of Dorset. There are of course more spectacular ones—that of Cornwall springs immediately to mind; but not one that possesses more variety in its composition.

Here you come to the westmost outlier of the great whaleback of chalk uplands that characterise East and West Sussex, much of Hampshire and much, too, of Berkshire and Wiltshire. Intermingled with this, often in fascinatingly complex fashion, is the harder oolitic limestone, that begins its north-eastwards march across England from the Dorset-Devon border by way of the Cotswolds and Northamptonshire, and continues on its way, with an occasional temporary lapse, to the North Sea at Scarborough and Whitby. There are other subsoils too—for instance, gravel, clay, and more friable soils over which extensive heathlands have established themselves. But fundamentally the coastline is one of alternating chalk and limestone. Jointly, these are responsible for the striking formations to be seen towards the eastern end, short of Poole Harbour.

Durdle Door, and Stair Hole in Lulworth Cove, are but two of the many strange rock formations in the shape of arches or stacks or twisted pinnacles that thrust their grotesque shapes out of blue water to startle all who encounter them for the first time. The first-named may be the more popular sight, being a great, rugged arch of limestone, also known as Purbeck 'marble', rising out of the water just off shore. But Stair Hole, which forms one concave side of the almost wholly enclosed Lulworth Cove near by, is the more impressive of the two; for it tells a story in visual form that is not often to be found in Britain generally, at least away from the west coast, where a parallel is to be seen near Bude, on the North Cornish coast. It is of intense interest to the geologist, for it presents in dramatic form, almost as in a gigantic museum show-case

19

Stair Hole, Lulworth Cove

impressive evidence of what can result from mass movement of solid rock affected by architectonic forces.

The action of the tides sweeping up and down the English Channel, impelled by the power of the Atlantic to the west and the bottle-neck of the Dover Strait to the east, has played strange tricks with all this coastline, though the only spectacular effects are to be found towards its eastern end. Poole Bay is a generously scooped-out portion of the coast, curving westwards and southwards from Hengistbury Head (on which prehistoric man had one of his earlier hill-forts) by way of Southbourne and Boscombe to Bournemouth, with a 'bubble' that forms the virtually land-locked Poole Harbour. Beyond this comes the huge rock mass forming the Isle of Purbeck, with Studland, Swanage, Durlstone Head and, finally, St Alban's or St Aldhelm's Head.

Westwards beyond this is the even greater sweep of Weymouth Bay, which fills the fifteen miles or so of gently curving coast to the sudden southwards thrust of Portland Bill, interrupted only by the small coves and minor bays, with their headlands, such as Lulworth, Worbarrow and Kimmeridge. Like the 'Isle' of Purbeck, Portland is not a true isle, though so called, but it comes much nearer to being one than Purbeck does. It is in fact a nodule of solid limestone; the source of the famous 'Portland Stone' used for pavement-slabs and building material in many parts of the country. About four miles long from north to south,

Durdle Door, nr Lulworth Cove

and barely two miles in width, it tapers off to a blunt tip with a light-house on it. But for the narrow causeway just wide enough to carry a road and protective wall, Portland would truly be an island.

It is a strange, even forbidding, place, and one that makes a powerful impact on the first-time visitor. The road to it lifts off the causeway that has carried it southwards from Weymouth. The massive grey walls of Castletown crowd in upon it on either side. They are in part prison walls, though the old convict prison is now a Borstal; other portions behind them belong to the Ministry of Defence.

The stone from this rock mass has of course been used for all the buildings, large and small. It was used also for the great naval harbour created in the middle of the last century, the hard labour being carried out by the convicts, who at that grim period wore the broad arrow of their attire and worked under the surveillance, if not the lash, of tough overseers. One can see a parallel here with the building of the pyramids

Portland Stone Quarry

Pulpit Rock, Portland Bill

by slaves in ancient times. This inexhaustible store of living rock has been consistently exploited from the reign of James I onwards. Once you get into the more open country, with its scanty tilth of soil and scrub (trees are practically non-existent), to the south of Castletown, you cannot look far in any direction without seeing at least the overgrown remains of one of the innumerable quarries. A few of them may still be in use, though many have now been abandoned; some of them have a stark beauty, while others possess a strange element of menace.

The sense of isolation from the main stream of life is as strong here as it is in, say, the Connemara district of Eire. It may well be that the inhabitants of the Isle of Portland are at heart as generous and hospitable as any in the homelier parts of Dorset, but there is a strong sense of deliberate withdrawal in the small-windowed, massively-built homes, and they do not exude the outgoing warmth that emanates from the thatched cottages in the main part of the county. The men, especially, are a tough breed, and probably their womenfolk too. Even Thomas Hardy wrote of the inhabitants of this stone peninsula: 'They are a curious and well-nigh distinct people, cherishing strange beliefs and singular customs.'

He did add that these beliefs and customs might be becoming obsolescent, but this was mere guesswork; he was a man of Wessex, not a Portland Islander.

I have returned to Dorset more times than I can count; but I have travelled along that narrow causeway only twice, and have no particular wish to do so a third time. The trip was worth it, however, for the chance to visit the old lighthouse near the point, or 'Bill'. It dates from the end of the eighteenth century, but has comparatively recently been adapted for the use of keen sea-bird watchers. Beyond it are two objects that catch the eye and haunt the memory long after the bleakness of Portland generally has been forgotten. One of these is the Shambles lightship, moored in one of the most dangerous stretches of water anywhere along our coastline. Dangerous because just here there is the continuous surge of what may be termed a dual tide-race. More vessels were lost in the days of sail in this reach of deceptively treacherous water than in any comparable area, not forgetting the area between the coast of Cornwall and the Isle of Scilly. The other feature is not man-made but natural; the high, triangular wedge of rock thrusting upwards and dubbed, perhaps with unconscious irony, the Pulpit Rock.

It is to the west of the Isle of Portland that the strangest (though not

Old Lighthouse on Portland Bill

Chesil Bank and Portland Bill

the most dramatic) length of the Dorset coastline is to be found. This is the unique phenomenon shown on the map as Chesil Bank; and it *is* unique, even in all Europe. Some eighteen miles in length, it follows the gentlest of curves from close to Portland Bill westwards to a point just south of Bridport. It is a huge bank of pebbles, subtly graduated in size from the largest, near Portland, to the smallest at the Bridport end. It is said that so consistent is the graduation that the old-time smuggler, and indeed a veteran inshore fisherman, could estimate his position at sea by the difference in the sound of the pebbles as they were rolled by the tides.

The Chesil Bank is vast not only in length but in breadth. At its widest it comes near to two hundred yards; at its eastern end it is more than forty feet high above high-water mark. For half its length it encloses two long, narrow lagoons known respectively as East and West Fleet. The keen observer, will notice that not only the size of these billions of pebbles varies from small to large, but their hue also varies. At the western end, close to where the oolitic limestone so familiar to us in Dorset and the Cotswolds predominates, the smaller pebbles have a warmish tinge; appropriately enough, closer to the old convict-worked Portland quarries, the larger pebbles take on a greyer hue.

Geologists and oceanologists and others have puzzled for generations over the problem of just why this extraordinary barrier of pebbles should have been thrown up, and maintained fundamentally unaltered

26

West Fleet, nr Abbotsbury

in appearance in spite of the variety of the Channel gales and the formidable weight of the tides sweeping eastwards and westwards along this gently curved stretch of coastline. Local legend has it that Chesil Bank 'appeared overnight' during a phenomenal storm, and that prior to this the Isle of Portland was truly an island, separated from the mainland by a tidal race as terrifying as that between the 'toe' of Italy and Sicily, where the mythical Scylla and Charybdis held sway. In an age when living volcanoes have appeared overnight, as for example off the southwest coast of Iceland, who can doubt that nature is capable of producing such phenomena? There are some who believe that if Chesil Bank could be thrown up in one night, then, as the result of some unparalleled storm, it could equally well be washed away overnight. In that case the friable chalk of the coastline behind it, even though buttressed by outcrops of limestone, would be completely at the mercy of the ever-restless, eroding tides. The people who make up the small communities of Wyke Regis, for example, and Chickerell, Langton Herring and Abbotsbury, and even the thriving resort of Weymouth, would then be in peril.

The coastline continues its scimitar-like curve westwards beyond Burton Bradstock, where some of the most impressive 'layer-cake' limestone cliffs rear up from the shingle, by way of the great headland suitably named Golden Cap, to Lyme Regis, within a mile or so of the Devon border. For many people—as the sprawling caravan sites of Seatown and other places along this beautiful stretch of cliff-dominated coastline emphasise—this is the best stretch of all. It possesses no seaside resorts of any size at all; Charmouth and Chideock (pronounced 'Chiddick') lie on the road that runs parallel with the coast a few miles inland. The 'layer-cake' formation of the cliffs is due to the alternating hardish limestone and in-filling of softer, more crumbling rock. This may be seen at its best from a boat lying off shore; but if the sun is nearly overhead and just a little to the west, impressive views can be obtained from, say, near Lyme Regis, looking eastwards to Golden Cap and the Burton Bradstock cliffs a few miles farther on. Golden Cap is the most outstanding of the headlands that have withstood the incessant wear-and-tear of the Channel waves.

As with Poole Bay and Weymouth Bay, Lyme Bay makes a more positive southwards turn as it approaches Lyme Regis, at the south-west-most limit of our county. The water is shallower here, the 5-fathom line being nearly a mile out from the shore. Dorset as a whole can claim, even in this latter end of the twentieth century, to be the most unspoiled county in all England, with Suffolk as its nearest rival. This little corner of it does contain a seaside resort and is therefore vulnerable to the threat of exploitation and commercialisation; yet it has miraculously contrived to maintain its integrity. We shall return to it in the next chapter. It is as complete a contrast as can be imagined to the vast urbanisation and sophistication of Bournemouth-with-Boscombe eighty miles distant along this coastline.

In addition to the unique Chesil Bank, and to the sheer beauty of the limestone cliffs, there is, especially for the geologist, whether professional or amateur, a wealth of interest in this coastline as a whole. At one end, the convoluted strata of Lulworth Cove's Stair Hole; and at the other end, around Lyme Regis, the chalk and oolitic limestone rock formations laid down when this part of Europe was submerged beneath sea water and now revealed. These, with their fossils and other relics from aeons past, are among the happiest of hunting-grounds for the hammer-wielding geologist.

There is clear evidence here of the existence in remote prehistoric times of creatures large and small that lived out their lives here. At Black Ven, for example, a mile or two along the coast from Lyme Regis, the fossalised remains of an icthyosaurus were found in 1811, by a child named Mary Anning. The enormous footprints of dinosaurs have been found; the vast bones of a plesiosaurus, and parts of the skeletons both of elephants and of crocodiles, to mention a few of the larger creatures only. The fossils of shellfish large and small abound, creatures that

Layer Cake' Cliffs, Burton Bradstock

crawled or swam untold eternities ago amid the roots of now petrified trees that also have been brought to light. The fortunate geologist, veteran or tyro, is almost certain to turn up something new if he or she perseveres with hammer, brush and trowel.

Those who are not disposed to undertake what can in fact be quite exacting labour, can see for themselves, without effort in local museums at Lyme Regis and Portland, exhibits that are the results of the dedicated labour of others. Portland museum, even if not the better of the two, has a special interest in that it was formerly the property of Marie Stopes, who permitted its conversion because it had been Avice's cottage in Hardy's novel, *The Well-Beloved*. Hardy had described it as 'like the Island, all of stone, not only the walls but in window frames, roof, chimneys, fence, stile, pigstie and stable'. It should be remembered that, before he became a novelist and author of *The Dynasts* and other poems, he had trained as an architect; his descriptions of buildings are always faithful down to the last unimportant-seeming detail.

29

One or two more points about this coastline should be added. Chalk and oolitic limestone often prove to be the breeding-grounds not only of fossils but of living creatures. The eastern end of these cliffs especially are rich in potential finds for the entomologist and the botanist alike. There is one exceptionally rare butterfly, which takes its name from a feature of the coastline that is more ordinarily the preserve of the geologist, Lulworth Cove. In fact, the Lulworth Skipper, as the entomologist knows it, is more likely to be found amid the foliage inland from Swanage, among the Purbeck Hills, than at the foot of that spectacular rock formation, Stair Hole.

Finally, a reminder that much of the cliff-top edge is deceptively dangerous to walk on, for the friable rock supporting the thin skin of grey-green turf is by no means always to be relied upon. Only the foolish walker treads right on the edge. It is worth remembering that on Christmas Day in the year 1839 an area of no less than forty acres on the Devon side of Lyme Regis collapsed without warning, to leave a chasm nearly a mile in length and 400 feet in width. This spectacular landslide has now been designated an official Nature Reserve; the catastrophe has been turned to good account.

3. Coastal Resorts

IT WAS ACTUALLY a Hampshire man, author of a comprehensive and exhaustive volume on his own county, who set down in cold print the uncompromising statement: 'The story of Bournemouth is a romance of Big Business, but it will never be history, unless it be the history of a ruined coastline... Bournemouth is quite a nice place but despite the fact that it holds an important position in modern English social history, it can be dismissed immediately from any book about Hampshire.'

An uncompromising statement indeed, and one that will perhaps be found a little off-putting. Though Bournemouth is now in Dorset, probably Eric Benfield, Dorset man to the core and author of a book on his county in the same classic series, would have written to much the same effect. A little unfair, surely? For Bournemouth with Boscombe has much to offer the visitor, particularly if he is looking for the well-groomed rather than the wild-looking.

A hundred and fifty years ago the ground over which the town has now spread was mainly marshland and moorland; such small houses as there were constituted what might be termed a marine village. The poorish soil, however, lent itself to the growing of conifers, and in the middle of the nineteenth century pines were planted here in their thousands, to form a radically different and more attractive environment. The site in any case looked due south; it was very soon completely protected from north winds by the vast acreage of swiftly-growing trees, and recognised as a God-given, man-enhanced sun-trap, it naturally grew apace. By the end of the century it had become a sizable town of about 40,000 inhabitants. Its natural warmth and growing air of sophistication drew more and more thousands to settle there, and has continued to do so to this day.

Bournemouth's forward-looking Corporation, with the willing co-operation of well-heeled citizens, set about increasing its natural amenities. Miles of open, sunlit beaches were there for the taking. Parks and public gardens and tree-shaded glades were added, two of them extending to nearly 200 acres each. There are now several museums. In addi-

tion to its excellent Marine Room, the Rothesay has an outstanding collection of pottery and porcelain; the Russell-Cotes also has a collection of fine porcelain, and a notable display of Japanese and Burmese art, collected over the years by a former lord mayor whose name the museum bears. Another display, of special interest to the geologically minded, is its collection of fossils and other finds from the Purbeck and other quarries. They are intelligently set out and identified on what is known as the Geological Terrace, and will certainly whet the curiosity and appetite of enthusiasts already bound for the Portland and Lyme Regis museums mentioned in the previous chapter.

For true history, however, you must go to Christchurch, a mile or so to the east, though now encompassed within the enlarged county, whose boundary-line runs down very close to its outskirts. It is happily

32

Bournemouth: Cherry trees

Boscombe Chine

placed between two rivers, the Avon (one of so many bearing this name) and the Stour, which has given its name to many Dorset villages during its leisurely course south-eastwards to its confluence with the Avon in Christchurch Bay. The town is ancient enough to have received mention in Domesday, in which, more than a thousand years ago, it was known as Twyneham.

In due course a minster church was built, and the name appropriately changed to the one it bears today. As with many of these ancient churches, and the communities they served, legends as to its founding are rife, and picturesque. Though no one today believes the story of the building of Christ's Church, originally on St Catherine's Hill overlooking the town that was to spring up, as usual, about it, it is one of the more picturesque of them. Bishop Flambard was its founder, and work was begun on it shortly after the Norman Conquest. But for all their dedicated perserverance, the builders were continuously frustrated; every morning when they arrived at day-break to continue with what they had abandoned at night-fall the day before, they found that their work had been undone and the stone and timber removed to a different site.

Disturbed by what appeared to be the work of some hostile agency, Bishop Ranulf Flambard knelt and prayed. He was told in a vision-dream that the site to which the materials were being transported during the hours of darkness was the one on which Christ wished His church to be built. So, work was recommenced on the new site, and from that day onwards went ahead without further hindrance. Confirmation of his dream came one day when some timbers that had been hewn from oak trees brought from the New Forest proved to have been wrongly measured and were too short to carry the roof. The carpenters laid down their tools in despair, faced with the formidable task of replacing them. Next morning, to their astonishment, every timber was found to be exactly the right length after all. Bishop Flambard, and doubtless the pious craftsmen who were working for him, felt convinced that Christ the Carpenter had personally intervened and solved their problem for them.

Over the years the church was added to, and became an Augustinian priory, which it remained for some four centuries until the Dissolution of the Monasteries by Henry VIII. The priory buildings were destroyed and the monks disbanded, as usual. But Christ's Church survived, and is in use to this day, as splendid an example of Norman craftsmanship as you are likely to find anywhere along the Channel coastline. Its nave is 118 feet long and there are seven true Norman arcades surviving, together with the crypt, which is wholly intact; the turret flanking the

Priory Church, Christchurch

north transept is regarded by experts to be among the finest examples of Norman craftsmanship in the whole country. The north entrance to the church was added a couple of centuries later, its beauty enhanced by the approach to it through an avenue of elm trees that replace the more customary yews. The reredos is a century later still, of exquisitely carved stone, but there is wood carving in the choir stalls that dates back to the thirteenth century; and even though this is confronted by some carving of the fifteenth century, it fully holds its own in beauty and intricacy.

Much more could be written about this church whose origin—if legend is to be accepted as truth—was so mysterious. The most beautiful features are probably the chantries, notably the Salisbury Chantry carved in stone taken, not from the Purbeck quarries but from Caen, in Normandy, stone that was used for so many of our own great edificies, including Canterbury Cathedral.

There is much more to be seen in the town. There are the remains of the castle keep, built early in the twelfth century but, as at Corfe, 'slighted' by Cromwell's Roundheads during the Protectorate. Associated with this are the remains of the 'Castellan's', or Constable's House, to be found in the garden of the *King's Arms Hotel*. Red House museum is a fine Georgian building, reminiscent of some of those in Blandford Forum. Older than this by many centuries is the Norman arched bridge spanning the Avon; and there are the remains, too, of the ancient mill that served the occupants of the priory in its heyday, its wheel turned by the water that flowed past it on its way to the harbour. This itself is dominated by Hengistbury Head, and is of course a favourite haunt of enthusiastic small-boat sailers.

Though not far distant in miles, it is a far cry indeed from the medievalism of Christchurch and the sophistication of Bournemouth, with its great hotels, tower-blocks of flats, multiple stores and esplanade, to the unpretentious red-brick seaside resort of Studland, just beyond landlocked Poole Harbour, and its larger neighbour, Swanage, three miles to the south up-and-over the thrusting spine of Ballard Down. Before we come to these, however, a word or two about Poole itself.

The town is not prepossessing, at any rate from the landward side; indeed, it could be regarded as a commercialised western outlier of Bournemouth. It derives its importance, essentially, from its spacious harbour, or rather interlocked series of harbour and sand-flats through which sinuous waterways flow, behind which it was built. The harbour entrance is so narrow that on any but a large-scale map it does not seem to exist at all. Its periphery is in the region of a hundred miles, though it seems to be not more than four miles across in one direction and less

Custom House, Poole

than that in the other. The explanation of this seeming paradox lies in the infinite number of inner harbour and harbour-lets, minor estuaries and other recesses. An oval mass of land a mile long by half a mile wide forms an island within this irregular frame, Brownsea Island. It is now, deservedly, a Wild Life Sanctuary in the care of the National Trust.

Poole Harbour has been a base for shipping, both legitimate and otherwise, since medieval times. So vital to Elizabeth I's interests did it prove to be that she designated it a 'county' in its own right, a unique status which it retained for some three hundred years. Vessels sailed from it to harass the shipping of France and Spain; buccaneers made use of it for their forays, and as a place to retreat to when pursued; for smugglers it proved an invaluable base at which to off-load their contraband. The maze of narrow waterways, which varied with every change of tide, revealing and alternately concealing sandbanks that could be used as hiding-places, presented an almost insuperable obstacle both to marauders from the English Channel and to the Revenue Men attempting to maintain the officialdom and authority of the Customs House. Poole, incidentally, was the base for the merchants who traded with Newfoundland, and many of the men who were among the first waves to establish a colony there, were from Poole who had salt in their bloodstream, and from near by Wareham, close to the perimeter of the harbour, and from Lytchett Minster, a few miles to the north-east but still within smell of salt water. Some were already master-mariners, other 'fore-the mast men.

Though much of the town is thoroughly modernised, combining the residential with the commercial, (shipbuilding and warehousing for coastal trade and also the traditional making of Poole Pottery still occupy many of its inhabitants) it is not difficult to track down features that date back to a much older age, even as far as medieval times. Blue Boar Lane, with its flagstones and central gully for running water, is an example of this. Scaplens Court, in Sarum Street, known also as The Town House, is of medieval origin, portions of it possibly dating back almost to the twelfth century, though the roof timbers were replaced, as is so often the case with very old buildings, some time in the fifteenth or early sixteenth century. Looking seawards along the dockside, you may catch a glimpse of a 3,000-ton cargo boat making for the narrow pincer-like harbour entrance. Turn around and indulge in a little exploration, and you quickly step back in time into an earlier age.

So to Studland and Swanage, the two seaside resorts that lie between Poole and St. Aldhelm's Head, on the eastern face of the Isle of Purbeck. Studland is the more modest of the two, though there is nothing

Purbeck Hills

Corfe Castle

pretentious about its larger neighbour a few miles to the south. It has its own little bay, sharing its name, which provides a base for the small-boat sailor who is happier away from the big conglomerations of yachts that require expert crews. Those using this bay, however, must exercise caution if the wind should veer to the east, blowing emphatically on-shore; the blunt cliffs of the Isle of Purbeck, whether predominantly fri-able chalk or the harder stone, are not suitable as land-falls by east-wind-driven small boats.

The great mass of the Isle of Purbeck, dominated by the ruins of Corfe Castle four miles inland from the coast, was a smugglers' haunt for many generations; the whole area, as the history books dealing with the smugglers' heyday clearly show, does not seem to have been con-tained within the jurisdiction of any specific authority. Indeed, this was the case as long ago as the sixteenth century, before smuggling reached its peak. There existed what was technically known as a 'Liberty', whose base was at the castle. Contraband was brought ashore at secret coves and caves by men who knew they were on to a good thing since the law had difficulty in touching them, even if its officers succeeded in locating them.

So notorious did this region become that even members of the nobility sent their servants, or occasionally appeared in person, probably incognito, 'to see what the smugglers had to offer'. Stories were rife that certain unnamed authorities were accepting bribes, in the form of valuable gifts of plunder, 'for goodwill and favour in the Island of Purbeck'. Gifts such as these covered a very wide range of goods; parrots from Brazil, ivory from West Africa, bracelets of Barbary gold, wine from Crete and, perhaps most surprising of all, hawks from Norway. This contraband obviously came from men who were pirates rather than mere smugglers, using larger vessels to sail the high seas; indeed, they operated much more openly, and with bravado.

Having these larger vessels, they could not really operate in any other fashion. So powerful were the captains, so numerous and ruthless their crews, that authorities were chary about attempting to quash their activities, even if they were strong-minded enough to resist the temptation to offer bribes. So far as the official 'Searcher' based in Poole, was concerned, he apparently held to the tenet, 'If you can't beat 'em, join 'em'. He did not actually sign on the dotted line, but he worked out a mutually satisfactory system whereby he obtained what he wanted in exchange, not for gold but for commodities which the ships' crews required. He offered powder and shot in exchange for wines; salt beef and bacon for silks and satins; live roes and bucks from the New Forest for spices from the Far East. It was a most satisfactory system of barter, whereby only the government of the day was the loser.

There were the rare occasions when the official attempted to make a stand, but he and his men were almost invariably defeated. There was one such occasion when he rallied his officers and actually set siege to Corfe Castle. The siege failed. In his report he stated: 'The crews who had come ashore were so strong and well appointed as they cannot of the sudden be repulsed'. And where were these well-appointed vessels dropping anchor? As often as not, right there in Studland Bay.

Essentially, little Studland is a seaside resort well suited to families with small children, but it has other features. The largely Norman church, dedicated to St Nicholas (patron saint of children as well as of mariners), is regarded by connoisseurs as among the finest, though not of course the largest, of its period in the whole of Dorset. It was built, almost certainly, on the site of a Saxon church, the relics of which no longer exist. But the Saxon foundations were utilised by the Normans, who built this church overlooking the flattish horseshoe of the bay. The low-lying, somewhat marshy heathland, extends beyond the northern fringe of the small resort to the southern fringe of Poole Harbour. It has

41

happily been designated a Nature Reserve, and the rambler may obtain a nature-trail leaflet and make his way without complications to the established observation-post, from which there is an infinitely varied selection of views both seawards and landwards. On large-scale maps you will read the words Agglestone and Puckstone, a furlong or two apart. They are not hamlets but two huge isolated stones, much eroded by wind and weather. The first-named is an enormous boulder nearly twenty feet high and reminiscent of the famous 'Bowder Stone' in Borrowdale, except that its setting could hardly be nore different. It is believed to weigh some 400 tons, and has of course accumulated about itself, as such monsters do over the centuries, innumerable myths involving Old Nick or some pagan god; they started long before written records were set down, so that each story-teller could embellish his version as he chose.

Swanage, nestling at the southern extremity of its own curving bay enclosed by Ballard Point and Peveril Point, was a base for the shipment of Purbeck stone from the quarries scattered about just inland long before it became a pleasant seaside resort. This was made possible by the construction of a railway-line that wound its way behind Poole Harbour to Wareham and Corfe, by-passing unimportant Studland, and ended abruptly at the water's edge. The place has a much earlier claim to importance. It was off this piece of coastline that King Alfred routed a marauding Danish fleet as long ago as 877 A.D. This very early naval engagement is anachronistically commemorated by a monument topped by four cannon-balls—which of course had never been thought of eleven centuries ago. Another unlikely monument in such a place is a clock-tower erected as a memorial to the Duke of Wellington. Why at Swanage? No one seems able to answer the question. The stone tower, in Gothic style, stood originally on an older London Bridge than the present one, and was transferred to this improbable site in the 1860s.

A far more unusual monument, and one that really attracts the sight-seer, is the Great Globe, not far from the Tilly Whim Caves, which were among the many used by the small-time smuggler, the result of quarrying very close to the cliff edge in olden times. It is in the various strata of limestone in caves such as these that some of the most interesting of the fossils have been unearthed; but for every one who goes to see the fossils in the various small, local museums, a hundred and more will go to see the Great Globe, and marvel at it.

It is indeed an extraordinary object: a sphere of grey Portland stone ten feet in diameter and weighing some forty tons. Representing the Earth, it is marked with the outlines of all the continents and oceans and

The Great Globe, Tilly Whim, Swanage

the lines of latitude and longitude and the equator. It is surrounded by stone slabs containing a variety of information. One of them informs you that, in comparison with this globe, the Moon would be only 33 inches in diameter, while the Sun would be 1,090 feet. Chunks of geographical information are interspersed with uplifting sentiments in both verse and prose quoted from Wordsworth, Milton, Tennyson, Shakespeare, Pascal and the Old Testament, and other sources. In addition there are sundry anonymous fragments of advice: 'Let Justice Be the Guide to All Your Actions', and 'Let Temperance Chasten You and Fortitude Support You'. The man who was responsible for this work of art was a local worthy, a not-so-Eminent Victorian. He was also lacking in the modesty which he recommended so earnestly to others, for he had

Old Harry Rocks, Swanage Bay

one of the stones inscribed with the odd and indeed incomprehensible statement that he 'also Made the Stars'.

The Great Globe and the Tilly Whim Caves are all within a stone's-throw of one of the Isle of Purbeck's most impressive promontories, Durlston Head, but there are others hereabouts that are individually impressive and memorable. Off-shore from Ballard Down, the eastwards end of the ridge that runs west-east along Purbeck, there is the group of grey-white stacks known as the Old Harry Rocks. These have their parallel in The Needles, off the western tip of the Isle of Wight. Like the more unusual formation, Durdle Door, they have so far

resisted the incessant erosion of the restless water. Looking westwards, the view from another of Purbeck's magnificent headlands, St Aldhelm's (or St Alban's) Head, is one that imprints itself on the memory.

So much for the cluster of seaside resorts at the eastern end of the 80-mile coastline that terminates at Lyme Regis, on the border with Devonshire. Midway along this curve is the seaside resort of Weymouth. At first sight it may give the impression of being wholly Victorian; in fact that impression is a false one. There is much in the town that is Georgian, and it was indeed George III who, so to speak, put the town on the map. It is suprising, and certainly irks the good citizens, that the King

45

View from St Aldhelm's Head

did not bestow upon the town the royal *cachet* of 'Regis', as George V did to Bognor. After all, George III was the first English monarch to 'take the waters' here, not by drinking from any mineral spring but, quite literally, by plunging into the quiet waters of Weymouth Bay.

The resort, which is also the base for cross-Channel ferries, claims to be the first in England to establish the use of horse-drawn bathing-machines which older readers may recall having seen, and possibly even used, in their childhood days. In 1789, to the martial strains of the National Anthem, this enterprising monarch had his specially con-structed 'machine' drawn well into the shallow water so that when he descended the wooden steps to wade up to his armpits his royal person would not be displayed to the vulgar eye. His medical advisers had told him that sea-water would effect a certain cure for the various maladies from which he suffered at the time. Indigestion may well have been the least of these, and sea-water, he was assured, could be relied upon to cure this. His rheumatism, too, would be eased at once, and probably cured for ever.

Whether this proved to be the case or not, Weymouth was grateful for the lead set by George III, and capitalised upon his example. People came from far afield to try out this wholly novel idea of plunging the per-son into sea-water. Bathing-machines appeared in whole flotillas over-night. Ladies were persuaded that if the royal body could entrust itself to these waters, then so could they—provided always that the activity could be indulged in discreetly, with a woman or two at hand to encom-pass them with large towels until they actually entered the water and to receive them in the same fashion as they mounted the two or three wooden steps to enter the privacy of the mobile hut in which they had discarded their raiment. In due course a statue to George III was erected on the esplanade, midway between the two piers, commemorating the connection between Weymouth and the monarch and, incidentally, as a tribute to his having completed his fiftieth year on the throne.

There is another memorial to him, but of a very different kind. As you take the road northwards in the direction of Dorchester, look across the shallow valley on your left near Osmington, two or three miles inland. There, carved out of the turf in gleaming white chalk and facing the morning sun, is George III on horseback, riding fast and furi-ous *away* from the resort where he had taken the waters in this unique fashion. Had he perhaps failed after all to benefit therefrom? Or had something occurred at the *Gloucester Hotel*, just behind the statue erected to him, at which he and his retinue were accustomed to stay when he visited Weymouth; something that had displeased the mon-

Weymouth Harbour

arch? No one seems able to answer that question; but the Weymouth Corporation would undoubtedly be glad if that equestrian figure were one dark night to turn about and thus give the impression that he was making as fast as he could for the pleasures of the town and the benefit of its water, rather than fleeing from it.

Weymouth can substantiate claims to having been in existence very much longer ago than during the reigns of George III and Victoria. It was used by the Romans for the off-loading of legionaries and their equipment when they were establishing themselves at Durnovaria, seven miles due north, for the great stone mass of Portland offered invaluable shelter from the prevailing westerlies that drove the waves eastwards up the Channel. The inexhaustible supplies of stone, too, were within easy reach for the building that went on during their occupation. Fifteen centuries later, Henry VIII, that great builder of coastal fortifications from Cornwall to Kent, recognised its value, strategically and otherwise, and caused Sandsfoot Castle to be built there to protect his shipping if and when need arose. It is true that there is now virtually nothing to be seen of his handiwork, but the fact remains that Weymouth had that sort of importance four centuries ago, even if it has tended to lapse in more recent times. Weymouth Harbour has been maintained as a base for both naval and merchant vessels ever since, and remains so to this day.

George III, nr Osmington

More picturesque by far, however, than the naval vessels and Channel ferries utilising the harbour—which, unlike Poole Harbour, is wholly man-made—is the open bay curving gently in front of the town and away from it to the north-east in the direction of Osmington. Tied up close in-shore are innumerable small yachts, and some not so small either, belonging to the members of Weymouth's very popular yacht club, which claims to be the nearest rival along the south coast to that of Cowes, on the Isle of Wight. (Lymington, over the Hampshire border, may challenge the claim!)

The whole town slopes comparatively steeply up and away from the water's edge, and there is no more attractive sight for miles in either direction than that formed by the movement of these many small sailborne craft seeking and making use of the winds that fan this curving stretch of coastline. The occupants of houses of the upper levels are

The Cobb, from E., Lyme Regis

indeed fortunate, being within little more than a long stone's-throw of the water, and therefore having something of a gull's-eye view of all that takes place in the bay. They are fortunate, too, in that their view is not marred by the ever-growing numbers of power-lines and their gaunt pylons that stride inexorably across the turf-clad downs behind them; or by the ever-increasing camping and caravan sites on this coast which, unless some responsible authority steps in soon, will have ruined all too many miles of this lovely coastline. It is good to see that already the National Trust has taken steps to thwart this deterioration.

One seaside resort, at the westmost end of this coastline, has happily remained almost totally unspoiled by the march of 'progress'—so often a euphemism for commercialisation and exploitation. Thanks largely to its situation, for it must be approached, whether from the east or from the west, by a steep, narrow and tortuous road, Lyme Regis has survived, small, cosy and unspoiled to this day. It has, however, a place in history, rather than in the prehistoric scene, though you would never guess this if you were not told in advance, for there is nothing overt to make the point. It was in Lyme Regis Bay that, in 1588, the first contact was made with the Spanish Armada, of which reports had been conveyed to Drake as he played bowls far to the west on Plymouth Hoe. In fact, no fewer than five of Drake's fighting vessels came from Lyme Regis. It already possessed the royal *cachet*, 'Regis', bestowed upon it six centuries ago by Edward I. It was a recognised port in the Middle Ages; it was also a centre of the cloth-making industry. During the Civil War it was a stronghold against the Royalists, and forty years later it

51

Sea Front Houses, Lyme Regis

was the beach-head on which the Duke of Monmouth landed preparatory to setting in train the rebellion he had instigated to topple the monarch James II from the throne.

The date was 11th June, 1685. Monmouth and his followers were rowed ashore in seven boats from a small fleet of vessels, the largest of which was the brig, *Helderenbergh*. They had come, as you can guess from the ship's name, from Holland. Monmouth's first act was to drop on to his knees and thank God for their safe arrival in the bay and to ask for a blessing on the task that lay ahead of them. He rose to his feet to find himself surrounded by, it would seem, every man in Lyme Regis, all crying out lustily: 'A Monmouth! A Protestant religion!' They rallied to his cause in every way. Small boats put out to assist in bringing ashore the equipment that would be needed for the battles he expected to have to fight, and indeed did fight at Sedgemoor and elsewhere, though he was not to be the victor. Lyme Regis men joined his ranks, leaving their looms and their boats to help him bring about the destruction of Popery in the land on which he was bent. They paid dearly for their loyalty: a dozen of them were publicly hanged at the very spot at which the Duke and his followers had come ashore—the famous Cobb. Monmouth himself was beheaded at the Tower of London on the

Sea Front Houses, Lyme Regis

orders of his uncle, James II, after a desperate attempt to escape by the way he had come.

The Cobb, quite apart from its historic interest, is the most outstanding feature of this small port, even if the charming terraced houses overlooking the curving esplanade are more immediately eye-catching. It is a massive stone-built curved wall, constructed as long ago as the year 1300 for the protection of fishermen's craft and the loading of small coastal vessels carrying cargoes of cloth and other goods. Today it curves about a flotilla of small pleasure-craft as well as such fishing-boats as are still in use. It juts out at the foot of yet another of the great cliffs that rear their heads to dominate many sections of Dorset's sweeping coastline. From this promontory, and indeed from the Cobb itself, looking eastwards you can obtain a splendid view of the greater promontory so well named, Golden Cap. Perhaps it was her delight in this view that brought near-disaster to Louisa Musgrove, in Jane Austen's novel, *Persuasion*. There is, however, as the text implies, a different and more foolish-romantic explanation.

Lyme Regis was the setting for much of this novel, and the author knew it well.

Louisa and Anne are walking on the Cobb with the handsome and

53

highly desirable Captain Wentworth. 'There was too much wind to make the high part of The Cobb pleasant for the ladies, and they agreed to get down the steps to the lower. All were contented to pass by quietly and carefully down the steep flight, excepting Louisa; she must be jumped down them by Captain Wentworth. In all their walks, he had had to jump her from the stiles; the sensation was delightful to her.' Louisa jumped, and was duly received into his arms. Not content with that, she must run up the steps a second time, to be jumped by him and once again be 'saved' by his manly arms.

He advised her against this, but she wilfully insisted. 'I am determined I will!' she exclaimed, and forthwith launched herself from the top. This time, however, 'she was too precipitate by half a second, fell on to the pavement of the Lower Cobb, and was taken up lifeless. The horror of that moment to all who stood around! Captain Wentworth knelt with her in his arms, looking on her with a face as pallid as her own, in an agony of silence. Mary screamed out "She is dead! She is dead!" and Anne cried out: "A surgeon!" ' But this is a romantic novel, and Louisa was by no means dead; all eventually was to end well. This time the Cobb had witnessed a landing, not by the Duke of Monmouth and his eager followers but by an impetuous, thoughtless young lady; literary history, perhaps, but not history in the true sense.

There is more to Lyme Regis, however, than the Cobb. Between it and the heart of the little resort there curves a modest esplanade, overlooked by some quite charming small houses of the Georgian period and style. From one of these doors, or from the wrought-iron balcony above, you would not really be surprised to see one of Jane Austen's characters—or even Jane herself—step out, parasol in hand to protect a delicate complexion from the strong sunlight or ozone-bearing sea breeze. Lyme Regis was a favourite haunt of the genteel citizens of Bath at the time of which she was writing; in essence, it remains today much as it was then; unassuming, welcoming, quiet and indeed serene.

There is a museum of more than purely local interest, housed in the late-Victorian-neo-Renaissance Town Hall. There is also the River Lym flowing steeply down, almost literally between the houses; in medieval times and later it powered the small cloth mills, some of which, now converted to private use as dwellings, are still to be seen. And there is the church, parts of which date back to the fifteenth century, though the west porch is in fact a relic of the Norman-built nave. Small as it is, Lyme Regis is full of surprises.

4. Dorchester, Sherborne and Shaftesbury

DORSET IS FORTUNATE in that no really major roads pass across her face. The great road to the West Country, the A30, linking London with Land's End, just impinges on her northern apex for a few miles between Shaftesbury and Yeovil, on her border with Somerset, so that traffic speeding between the metropolis and the Atlantic does not automatically pass through the county. This, for all who love Dorset, is as it should be. True, the map indicates main roads linking Salisbury with Dorchester, Wareham with Bridport, Dorchester with Sherborne, and Yeovil with Dorchester; but though the Ministry of Transport may classify these as major roads, they are Dorset examples of such roads, and have for the most part a character all their own.

Nor, apart from Bournemouth-with-Boscombe, Poole and Weymouth, are there any large towns—and these are small in comparison with the truly large towns of other counties, such as Bristol or Bradford or Birmingham. Dorchester, the County Town, has only some 14,000 inhabitants; Sherborne about 9,000; Bridport less than 7,000, Wimborne just over 5,000, Shaftesbury just over 4,000 and Blandford Forum, in spite of its impressive name, less than 4,000, and so on down the scale, until town has become township and township diminished to village and hamlet, as we shall see in a later chapter.

Dorset has no industries, as the term would be understood in the industrial Midland or North Country. Rope was once made in Bridport, and for many years the hangman's noose was jocularly known as a 'Bridport dagger'. Shaftesbury was once known for its manufacture of buttons, but was little more than a cottage industry, and is long since defunct. Portland and Purbeck still have their quarries, even if these are now worked on a smaller scale. Fundamentally Dorset is an agricultural county, and likely to remain so for the foreseeable future.

The County Town, as the name Dorchester implies, is of Roman origin, a *castra* on the road they constructed to link Salisbury (their Sarum) with Exeter far to the west. Only the expert can discern the remains of that original road on the east side of the town, for it is almost completely obliterated by farmland and the odd hamlet such as Winterborne Kingston. It joins the main A35 close to Tolpuddle, six miles distant, and the join is no longer discernible. But the A35, having once crossed the Frome, which was a wide-flowing stream with marshland on either side and so must have presented problems to the Roman engineers, now cuts a clean, straight swathe between the grey stone buildings that front on to East and later West High Street and continues on, straight as a die, as was the Romans' practice, for several miles before bearing southwards and leaving the original Roman road on which it was laid.

With so ancient an origin, you might expect in the Roman's Durnovaria a strong element of medievalism; this proves to be the case in Chester, for example, and in York. But if you look for this element, you will be disappointed. For much of the town that had grown up after the departure of the Romans in the fourth century was destroyed by a series of three major fires that occurred between 1613 and 1725, and, for good measure, a fourth that swept through the partly restored town just half a century later. Under a newer name, from which its present name obviously derives, Dorceastre, it became a Saxon town of some importance. Athelstan, grandson of Alfred, King of Wessex, had thought fit to establish a mint here—a comparatively rare distinction in those days and indeed for many years to come. There was a Norman castle, at which King John is known to have stayed in or about the year 1200, using it as a hunting-lodge when he was indulging in that sport in Cranborne Chase. But you will have to look hard indeed to find any relic of that castle, or of the friary that was established round about the same time; they have vanished without trace.

In medieval times Dorchester was a market town, as indeed it is to this day; it was well known for the ale brewed there, and for the manufacture of cloth, but those four great fires destroyed virtually every sign of medieval Dorchester. Alone among the old churches, that of St Peter survived, though it was badly damaged by the first of the fires, which broke out in the highly flammable premises of a tallow chandler. Much of the restoration of the church, though not all, was carried out in Victorian times. What you see in the town today, apart from the residential buildings spreading their anomalous red brickwork out along the roads that radiate from the centre in all directions, is in the main grey stonework, some of which did survive the fires but much of which has replaced the earlier buildings.

It is possible to locate a few surviving relics of the Roman town, which was founded about 70 A.D. and occupied for the better part of three hundred years. As usual, they walled the town, and small sections of this wall—not comparable with those at York, let alone those that encircle Chester—can still be located, notably in the area generally known as the West Walks. The Romans, however, are not responsible for the fine stands of elms to be seen in this area; they are said to have been planted by French prisoners during the Napoleonic Wars, in gratitude for kindnesses received from the warm-hearted citizenry.

Thomas Hardy was more acutely conscious of the Roman tradition than any visitor today is likely to be. 'It announced,' he wrote, 'old Rome in every street, alley and precinct. It looked Roman, bespoke the art of Rome and concealed the dead men of Rome. It was impossible to dig more than a foot or two deep about the town's fields and gardens without coming upon some tall soldier or other of the Empire who had lain in his silent unobtrusive rest for the space of fifteen hundred years.' He was writing of the town he called 'Casterbridge'. The visitor today must use his imagination; Hardy, writing a century ago, could use his powers of observation only slightly enhanced by his poetic gift, for in his day there were in truth fields and gardens very much closer to the centre of the town than they are today.

No, Dorchester looks what it is: a small County Town whose older buildings were constructed of the greyish Portland stone from that inexhaustible quarry not ten miles to the south. It has manifest composure, even dignity. Its main street is close-beset by dignified houses and offices standing shoulder to shoulder, and a number of inns and small hotels, notably *The King's Arms*, an important staging-post in the eighteenth century and later, and still the haunt of those who enjoy a good meal in spacious, restful and not too highly modernised surroundings.

As you climb the long slope of the High Street, from Grey's Bridge spanning the Frome to what is picturesquely as well as accurately known as 'Top o' Town', you have buildings of interest on either side of you. It is best to work along the street from west to east in the afternoon and early evening, for if the sun is low, with the road rising all the time, you have it full in your eyes. More normally, you would probably explore the centre of the town from Grey's Bridge, climbing gently all the way. Almost at once, you will find yourself with All Saints' Church on your left, facing the Corn Exchange and Town Hall on your right; just above these is St Peter's Church, with its memorial to the Dorset poet, William Barnes, a statue that seems at any moment about to step on to the narrow pavement.

Elbow to elbow with the church is the County Museum, one of quite exceptional interest even though (or perhaps because) it is devoted primarily to artefacts from the district. Here you will find a good display of the type of fossils that have been unearthed in the Purbeck and Portland quarries and elsewhere near by. There are a number of exhibits from prehistoric times, such as axe-heads and sling-shots. There are relics of the Roman and Romano-British period and, from a much later age, man-traps and other devices that came into their own when, as for so many generations, poachers of fish and game operated in great numbers.

The most interesting feature of this small museum, however, certainly for those who know the Wessex novels, is the reconstruction of Thomas Hardy's study as nearly as possible as it was in the home that he built for himself on the southern outskirts of the town, Max Gate. In the Hardy Room you can see the desk at which he wrote so many of the novels and short stories. At that desk he brought to life his tragic heroine, Tess; those memorable comics who formed the Mellstock Quire in his simple, romantic novel, *Under the Greenwood Tree*, a pastoral story with its echo of Shakespeare through which so many people first discover the *corpus* of Hardy's work. Here, too, was conceived Michael Henchard who, as a young hay tresser much the worse for drink, sold his new bride for five guineas, became the mayor of Casterbridge in the novel of that title, quarrelled with his rival in the corn trade, Donald Farfrae, and died pitifully in a hovel on Egdon Heath.

Hardy's Desk, Dorchester

On that desk you can see Hardy's leather-cornered blotting-pad and the pens he used to limn such characters as the capricious Eustacia Vye, the humble reddleman, Diggory Venn, the self-effacing Thomasin Yeobright and the violent and aptly named Damon Wildeve, and others who acted out their sombre parts in what many consider to be the finest novel of them all, *The Return of the Native*. Jude Fawley, too, was created at this desk and with one of these pens, protagonist in what his creator called 'a deadly war waged with old Apostolic desperation between flesh and spirit'. The appearance of *Jude the Obscure* in 1895 caused an uproar among serious readers, even Hardy's devotees; it would seem that even the author felt that he had now gone too far with torment, death and despair, for it was the last novel he was to write. The simple, bleak message found in the cupboard containing the hanged children, 'Done because we are too many', is among the most poignant phrases in English literature. The desk and its paraphernalia evoke the writer in detail: his magnifying-glass, his wallet, his paper-knife, his inkwell and letter-balance; and, perhaps most intimately, the pince-nez that perched on his thin, aquiline nose as he read and wrote.

It is an interesting fact that the 15th-century Church of St Peter adjoining the County Museum was restored in Victorian times by a Dorchester architect to whom Hardy had recently been articled, when his intention had been to become one himself; in fact, he was responsible for some of the restoration work. A more impressive memorial to him, however, is to be found a few hundred yards farther up High West Street, at its junction with The Grove and overlooking the roundabout that now facilitates the movement of east- and west-bound traffic into and out of this sword-blade thoroughfare. It is the work of Eric Kennington, war-time artist and sculptor. The statue portrays Hardy seated on a massive block of stone, his legs crossed and his hands clasping a crumpled hat on his knee. Sitting there on his plinth, coincidentally 'beneath a greenwood tree', he is just far enough removed 'from the madding crowd' to give the impression of isolation and deep, almost certainly sombre, thought. The tree throws light shadows over him, with an almost protective gesture. There is a simplicity about this memorial stone that echoes that of his Max Gate study reproduced in the County Museum just down High West Street. The inscription, too, is as simple as it could well be: Thomas Hardy 1840-1928. For those of us who know his work and recognise his quiet genius, nothing more is needed.

We have broken off our progression up the High Street, but will return to it anon, for there are other buildings of interest. For the

moment we will remain with Casterbridge's greatest citizen. He was born in a thatched cottage in a hamlet named Upper Bockhampton, in the shallow Frome Valley a couple of miles to the east of the town. It is a twin of the village of Lower Bockhampton, and it is at the crossroads between them that we meet the Mellstock Quire, bound for the house of Dick Dewey, where some of the rare passages of rustic entertainment in Hardy's novels are to be found. The rustics talk very much as do the comics in *A Midsummer Night's Dream*, though of course their dialect is that of the West Countryman. Stinsford is Hardy's Mellstock; he called Blandford Forum *Shottsford*, Swanage *Knollsea*, Sturminster Newton *Stourcastle*, Puddletown *Weatherbury*, Corfe Castle *Corvesgate;* and so on.

He was closely associated with Dorchester and its immediate environs for the whole of his long life—eighty-eight years. The cottage in which he was born lies at the end of an unmetalled track, so overshadowed by full-grown trees that it is difficult to photograph save for a brief period in a summer's day. He lived, and died, in a house he designed and built for himself in a secluded spot just off the road to Weymouth (his Budmouth), a mile or so from the centre of the town. At his express wish, his heart was buried in the churchyard of Stinsford, even though his ashes lie in Westminster Abbey, as befits a great writer of both prose and verse.

Back now to High West Street. The commemorative statue to William Barnes shows the old clergyman standing on a plinth considerably more ornate than Hardy's near by. Few would challenge the assertion that Barnes is the best dialect poet produced by England, comparable perhaps with Scotland's Rabbie Burns. He was writing poems before Hardy was born, and the two men became friends—in so far as anyone could establish such a relationship with a man so withdrawn as Hardy. Though Barnes was born in Blackmoor Vale, in the extreme north of the county, he spent most of his life in or near Dorchester. He was not out of his teens when he published his first slim volume of dialect verse, paid for by the sale of woodcuts he had been making as a hobby.

Hardy's Grave, Stinsford

Hardy's Birthplace, Upper Bockhampton

He came to Dorchester to live as a young man in 1835, half a decade before Hardy was born, and in fact lived for a number of years in a house next door to the architect John Hicks who had taken Hardy on as a pupil. In 1862 he was offered a living at the minute hamlet a couple of miles to the south-east of Dorchester, Winterborne Came. There he spent the remaining twenty-four years of his life in the little thatched rectory, writing his sermons and his dialect verse in a truly rural retreat. A pathway leads across the fields from the main road a mile or so east of the town and is the pleasantest and certainly the most appropriate means of access to this old-world spot.

Hardy loved him for the good man that he was, in a world in which, as the novels demonstrate, there was so much evil and man was so much at the mercy of the gods, 'who kill us for their sport'. Barnes came frequently from his isolated rectory to see the world go by in the High Street where now his statue stands. Hardy recalls his appearance on these occasions: 'An aged clergyman, quaintly attired in caped cloak, knee-breeches and buckled shoes, with leather satchel slung over his shoulders and a stout staff in his hand. He seemed usually to prefer the middle of the street to the pavement, and to be thinking of matters which had nothing to do with the scene before him, plodding along with a broad, firm tread, notwithstanding the slight stoop occasioned by his years ... Every Saturday morning, his little grey dog at his heels, he would halt opposite the public clock, pull out his old-fashioned watch from its deep fob and set it with great precision to London time.' Barnes was a character who might have stepped straight out from the pages of almost any one of those novels.

He lived to the age of eight-five, dying when the novelist was at the height of his powers, in 1886, the year that saw the publication of *The Mayor of Casterbridge*. One of the last verses that he wrote—or rather dictated, for he was by then too weak to hold pen to paper—is a moving reference to death, which was to be his lot so soon after, and to the effect that death has on those who still live:

> *And oft do come a saddened hour*
> *When there must goo away*
> *One well belov'd to our heart's core,*
> *Vor long—perhaps for aye;*
> *And Oh! it is a touchen thing*
> *The loven heart must rue*
> *To hear behind his last farewell*
> *The geate a-vallen to.*

Hardy and Barnes were figures revered in their time, and one of them loved also. But this same High Street was the setting for the activities of a man for whom, in his own day and ever since, loathing has been felt; and, in his day, fear and hatred at their most powerful. This was the infamous Judge Jeffreys, Jeffreys of the Bloody Assizes. His lodgings were in High West Street, at the back of premises which now form a restaurant; the old Court House over which, on his circuit, he presided, is an oak room to be found at the rear of *The Antelope*, yet another of the grey stone buildings that line this mounting street. There, in 1685, at the time of Monmouth's abortive revolution, he perfunctorily tried and summarily condemned to death 292 wretched prisoners. He was a sadist of a type hardly known in England in his time. As he went from Assize to Assize throughout Dorset he seemed anxious only to find as many victims as possible and to inflict on them the heaviest conceivable punishment.

A contemporary account records that 'some places (in Dorset) were

High West Street, Dorchester

quite depopulated and nothing to be seen in them but forsaken walls, unlucky gibbets and ghostly carkases. The trees were loaden almost as thick with quarters (human limbs) as leaves; the houses and steeples covered as close with heads as at other times with crows. Nothing could be liker Hell than all those parts; nothing so like the devil than he, Jeffreys. Caldrons hizzing, carkases boyling, pitch and tar sparkling and glowing, blood and limbs tearing and mangling, and he the great director of all.' Swift death by butchery could be replaced by torture that would almost certainly result in death. At Jeffreys' command, a fourteen-year-old barber's boy was ordered to be 'whipped throughout the market towns of the county every Saturday'; he was just one of an untold number of Dorset men, women and children who felt the power of James II through the intermediary of Judge Jeffreys of the Bloody Assizes.

High West Street was the setting, too, for the scandal of the sentences passed a century and a half later on the Tolpuddle Martyrs, though Jeffreys of course was long since dead. The chair he had occupied when holding his Assizes in Dorchester has been removed to the town's Council Chamber, where it may still be seen, together with the table on which he rested his arms while coldly, calculatingly then passionately he pronounced his dreadful sentences. This Old Shire Hall and Crown Court, on the opposite site of the street from Jeffreys' lodgings, saw the sentence of seven years' transportation passed on six farm labourers from the district around Tolpuddle, seven miles or so to the east of Dorchester.

Led by a local Wesleyan Methodist preacher named George Loveless, they had formed what must have been the first Trade Union in this country, The Friendly Society of Agricultural Labourers. Their claim was a very modest one: that their weekly wage should be raised from nine shillings to ten. As an immediate result, that already pitifully low wage was reduced to seven shillings a week, as a first warning against what was deemed intolerable insubordination. But the men—all credit to them—held firm. They were therefore arrested and made to march the seven miles to the Court House. This was in 1834, when transportation for life could be the sentence for stealing a sheep and even a small child could be publicly thrashed for petty theft.

The men were sentenced to transportation in prison hulks to Botany Bay, Australia. And there they might well have remained for life had not the citizens of Dorchester themselves, led by their own M.P., raised such an outcry that the sentence was reduced to two years and the men granted that cold comfort known even to this day as a 'free pardon'.

There were two lesser outcomes from this horrendous episode. The Trades Union Congress purchased the Crown Court in the Old Shire Hall as a public memorial; it also had built in the hamlet of Tolpuddle itself a row of six cottages for the express use of deserving agricultural labourers; these overlook the open space on the opposite side of the road with its memorial shelter and 'Martyrs' Tree'.

There is a great deal more that could be written about Dorset's County Town. The row of small buildings, for instance, known as Napier's Almshouses, dating from the early seventeenth century and now largely converted into shops. The castle-gatehouse-like building just beyond Top o' Town which is the headquarters and museum of the Dorset Regiments. It will probably surprise you to find, among the many trophies of a more obvious kind, the desk used by Hitler before and during World War Two. There is St George's Church, a stone's-throw from Grey's Bridge at the eastern entrance to the town, which survived the series of great fires that destroyed so much of the town during the late seventeenth century. Its tower dates from the fifteenth century, but its great treasure is the tympanum in the south porch, believed to date from about 1100 A.D., depicting the saint to whom the church is dedicated coming to the assistance of the crusaders in their campaign against the infidel. There is, too, an even more memorable feature, though experts are inclined to doubt the truth claimed for it. This is a tombstone that allegedly lies over the remains of a Roman named Gaius Aristobulus, who is known to have been an associate of St Paul. If—as does not really seem likely—this is the case, then we have here in a small medieval church on the edge of the town a positive link with the founders, nineteen centuries ago, of Dorchester-Dorceastre-Durnovaria.

If you are passing hurriedly through some town you will probably recall no more of it than a general impression of its superficial appearance. The silver-grey granite of Aberdeen is an example of this; the half-timbering of Shrewsbury is another; the red brick and stone quoins of Georgian and Victorian Leamington Spa is another, too. And certainly the cold grey Portland stone of Dorchester's High Street buildings leaves an impression of chill, even of austerity; you have to linger and explore to obtain other and more worthwhile impressions. How different, though, is the immediate impact of Sherborne, the ancient capital of the county and one of the most beautiful townships in all England.

It is to be found very close to the Somerset border, in one of the most angled of the innumerable crooks and turns that constitute this boundary-line, so strong a contrast with the smooth, gentle curve of that seaward boundary. Sherborne is sixteen miles almost exactly due north of

Dorchester, twenty-five miles from Portland Bill. It lies in the valley of the Yeo, with hills and downland to the south, east and north. Even from a distance, as you approach it from whatever direction, it seems to glow, to exude an ~~aura~~ that almost completely surrounds it. A little imaginative, perhaps? But not altogether far from the truth, for the greater part of the town is built of the beautiful yellow-ochre-near-golden limestone from the Ham Hill and other adjacent quarries. This raw material of its main buildings, as with the limestone of the Cotswold towns and villages, imparts to Sherborne a unity of conception as well as, more obviously, a feast for the appreciative eye. It has often been referred to as 'Dorset's show-piece'; such glib descriptions are often suspect, but, like the phrase or not, here it is fundamentally true. Nor has the town, like Bourton-on-the-Water in the Cotswolds, been commercialised and spoiled.

It was a cathedral city as long ago as 705 A.D., and remained so until

Sherborne Abbey Vaulting

1075, when the extensive diocese of Winchester was divided into two and the see was transferred to Old Sarum, now Salisbury, in neighbouring Wiltshire. Its first bishop was Aldhelm, later canonised, whose name is remembered now on that promontory of the Isle of Purbeck, St Aldhelm's Head. A century and a half after the founding of the first cathedral on this site it was taken over as their abbey church by the monks who established a monastery here. As so often, friction developed between the monks and the townfolk and the latter attacked the church and other buildings, destroying parts of them by fire. The reasons are not far to seek, for, as in most regions where monastic establishments held sway, the peasantry were required to pay tribute in various forms in exchange for the good offices of the monks, which were not always understood, let alone appreciated.

The original cathedral, then the abbey church, underwent much rebuilding during the thirteenth and subsequent centuries and came to its present splendid proportions and appearance as late as the fifteenth century. Its immediately most striking feature is the great vaulted roof of Ham Hill stone, one of the most perfect of its kind not only in Dorset but perhaps in all England. Ironically, it was because of a major fire that destroyed the timberwork of the older abbey church, when the townsfolk were yet again registering their hostility, that this noble roof was built, in the fifteenth century; out of evil, for once, came good.

Much of the abbey church, however, is very much older. There is the great tower, for example, which is largely Norman, as are the transept arches. Experts believe, though they have not yet succeeded in proving, that many if not all of the main piers, constructed in Perpendicular style, may have at their core piers which actually date from pre-Norman times. And you can go back yet further in history even than this, for you will find in the west wall a genuine Anglo-Saxon doorway. Confirmation of the fact that there was a Saxon church of real importance on this site is emphasised by the presence beneath the floor of the Lady Chapel of the tombs of two Saxon kings, Ethelbald and Ethelbert, who both reigned during the later part of the ninth century.

If the exterior of this great church is immediately striking for its richness of tone, its interior is even more rewarding in its detail. In strong contrast to the richly hued stonework of the main fabric, the many tombs and monuments, notably the effigies of the abbots of the monastery from the thirteenth century onwards, are sculptured in the greyer Purbeck stone that is so distinctive a feature of this and other, often quite small, Dorset churches. There are, too, a number of canopied 'altar tombs' to members of several important local families who throve in the sixteenth century, including the Horseys who contrived to 'inherit' the monastery buildings at the time of the Dissolution.

Though the choir stalls have been to a large extent renewed, many of them retain their original seats. Inspection of the misericords, as choir-stall seats are known, is always worth while indulging in, whether the church is large or small. Misericords are the hinged seats so designed that they could be sat on at need but also used as a partial support to the user when he was standing—a concession to the aged or infirm occupant of the stall. It would seem that the medieval craftsmen who were responsible for these stalls were often men with a sense of humour additional to the piety and the skill they necessarily possessed.

Whole books have been written about the immense variety of these carvings on misericords, which of course are always on the underside of the massive oaken seats. The ones in the abbey church at Sherborne are as interesting and attractive as any. Examine them in detail, and at your leisure, and you will come across memorable oddities. Beneath one of them, for instance, there is a carving of a powerful man engaged in a wrestling bout with a grotesque lion; another shows a small boy receiving no doubt well deserved chastisement; yet another shows a monkey busily devouring a heap of acorns. All these, like the others, date from the fifteenth century, when much of the finest oak carving was executed in our churches up and down the lands.

Sherborne School is one of the more famous of our smaller public schools, and also one of the oldest. Certainly there was a school here as long ago as the eighth century, and it is known that Alfred the Great, King of all Wessex, was a pupil here. The original buildings, of course, no longer exist, but the present school, apart from its later additions, occupies three at any rate of the original abbey buildings. It is to be found immediately to the north of the abbey church, its chapel having been the abbot's hall; as a school it was re-founded in the middle of the sixteenth century, some twelve years after the Dissolution of the abbey at the dictate of Henry VIII, but a good deal of additional building took place in the seventeenth century, all of which blends excellently with the earlier parts, as indeed does most of the building that has taken place as the school expanded in more recent years.

Of all the streets in Sherborne, without question the most interesting, the one with the greatest concentration of medieval buildings large and small, is Cheap Street. The name itself suggests buying-and-selling and marketing, as in Cheapside, London, and the innumerable 'Chippings' among our medieval market towns such as Chipping Norton and Chipping Ongar. It slopes steeply past the east side of the abbey buildings.

Here you will find the Hospice of St Julian and the Abbey Conduit, the latter virtually unchanged in appearance from what it was when constructed as a wash-house for the monks. It probably dates from the late fourteenth century, and in addition to the beautiful stonework there is some later but wholly integrated half-timbering. The tower of the abbey church rises nobly above the heavy-tiled roof with its near dormer windows.

There are other streets in Sherborne that merit a leisurely and rewarding stroll. Hound Street, Half Moon Street and The Green all have small and not-so-small buildings that catch and hold the eye. You have not far to walk (it is frustrating and indeed virtually useless to try to drive a car through these streets, twisting and narrow and often steep, with the frequent hazard of 'One Way Only') to find, for example, the 17th-century schoolhouse, the abbot's kitchen, and the library. Not far away, either, in this small town is the later school, known as Lord Digby's, built in the early part of the eighteenth century and so a mere upstart in comparison with Sherborne School itself; but it is worth a visit none the less. It dominates Newland, and among other claims to distinction was for a time the home of the famous actor William Macready. Long Street is noteworthy for its much later houses, of the Georgian period of architecture, which are to be seen in even greater profusion in Blandford Forum.

On the fringe of Sherborne to the east there are, though they are all too often overlooked by the casual passer-through, two castles. Known as The Old and The New, neither may be said to be particularly impressive as a castle. The first is almost entirely in ruins. It was built in the very early years of the twelfth century by Bishop Roger, Chancellor to Henry I, and survived for a few centuries until it became the object of attack by Cromwell's men. It was besieged twice before its garrison capitulated; then, as was his wont, the Protector (sic) had it slighted—which amounted to its being almost completely destroyed. Recently, work on it has been undertaken by the Department of the Environment, but it will never be possible to see it again as it was when it was completed in or about 1140 A.D.

The so-called New Castle is a different matter altogether. It is separated from its neighbour by parkland which was landscaped by 'Capability' Brown, complete with lake. It was largely built by Sir Walter Ralegh on an estate granted to him by Queen Elizabeth I in 1594, when he was still in her favour. He had in fact intended to refurbish the Old Castle, then owned by the Bishop of Salisbury, but was relieved of this onerous and probably non-productive task when he was granted the favour by his sovereign. He had, as always, big ideas. He would make his new home an object of wonder. It should have four towers and, as so often with Tudor buildings, a large number of chimney-stacks. As is well known, however, he fell into disgrace, and what he had designed as a permanent home passed into the hands of the Earl of Bristol. He had even more grandiose ideas and was to add four more towers and four wings to the original fabric.

To this day, and partly for this reason, it remains undistinguished in style and interesting chiefly for its connection with its original builder. There is a tradition that it was here beneath his own roof that Sir Walter was seen by one of his men-servants smoking a pipe of the tobacco he had brought back with him from Virginia—the country he named after 'the Virgin Queen', obviously with an eye to the main chance. His servant was so shocked, believing his master to be 'on fire', that he promptly threw the contents of a flagon of beer over him to extinguish it. History does not relate what the victim did to punish the offender, but those were harsh days, and the wretched fellow may well have lost his head, literally, as his master was to do in the Tower of London years later, in 1618.

Sherborne looks beautiful, as has been said, from all directions, and notably from the north and the south, for then the viewpoint is high above the valley in which it lies, sloping mainly southwards to the Yeo. But of the two main viewpoints, the better is the one from the south, for then the sun is behind you and lighting up the golden stone walls of the little town, distracting attention from the suburbs which, as with almost every town large or small in the land, are spreading outwards in ever widening congeries of buildings. Not all of these by any means are, alas, wholly in keeping with the essential Sherborne, the old part, with its medieval monastic and scholastic character and atmosphere, as perfectly integrated as any that come readily to mind. As I have written elsewhere, in a comprehensive book on England of which Dorset forms only one small section: 'Wherever the reader may start his peregrinations among the infinite resources of this county, Sherborne is the magnet towards which he must be irresistibly and most rewardingly drawn'.

Most towns, for obvious reasons, were founded at some point where a river could be crossed with comparative ease, as well as supplying water. This was usually done by way of a ford (hence the multiplicity of place-names containing this suffix: Bradford, Stratford, Stamford, Oxford and countless others); in due course a bridge would be built to make river crossings practicable in times of flood. Like Malvern, in the county newly named Herefordshire and Worcestershire, Shaftesbury is

Gold Hill (from top), Shaftesbury

an exception to this rule. It is one of the very few towns, unique in Dorset, that may be truly termed 'hill towns'. It stands on an escarpment some 700 feet above sea level that affords a magnificent view westwards and south-westwards over Blackmoor Vale, watered by the upper reaches of the Stour and its small tributaries and with the undulating contours of the high Bell and Woolland hills some twelve miles distant. This view, from the top of Gold Hill, given clear weather without haze, can be quite breathtaking.

Like Sherborne, Shaftesbury is a town of very ancient origin, dating back certainly to Saxon times. Its name was then Sceaftesbyrig, a typically 'portmanteau'-like word similar to those to be found across the Welsh border and meaning 'a fortified settlement at the end of a promontory'. The name is apt enough, as you will find out for your breathless self if you have climbed the formidable Tout Hill, on foot, that carries the road into the town from the south-west. The approach is certainly easier, if duller, from the south-east.

King Alfred took a hand in rebuilding what survived the ravages of the Danes. He founded a nunnery there, and appointed his daughter,

Aethelgiva, its first abbess, in 880 A.D. She was buried in the abbey church where, almost a century later, the body of King Edward the Martyr, murdered at the tender age of eighteen at the instigation of his stepmother, was brought from Corfe Castle by way of Wareham for burial in this hill town. Queen Aethelgiva, wife of Edmund of Ironside (as a forename it seems to have been popular among the Royals of that period), was also buried there. It was Alfred's grandson, Athelstan, who established no fewer than three mints here, in which silver coins bearing the name of the town were struck; these flourished until the year 1272, an unusually long life for such institutions.

Indeed, the whole town flourished exceedingly in pre-Norman times, and for many years afterwards. The Normans enlarged the abbey, using stone from the already famous Chilmark quarries. This stone is warmer in hue than the cold grey that characterises so much of Dorchester, but it never reaches the full glory of the Ham Hill stone that is to be seen at its best in Sherborne. The nunnery, or abbey, of course did not survive the Dissolution, any more than others did throughout the length and breadth of the land. Even during its heyday it may not have been as good an example of monastic discipline as it should have been. There are records of nuns being 'stolen' from it—possibly not altogether against their will. In one of these cases a lusty individual succeeded in abducting two nuns at one fell swoop. This was in the year 1285, long after the demise of Alfred's daughter. He was duly apprehended and brought up for sentence. You might think that such blatant interference in the even tenour of monastic life would have brought upon the offender dire punishment. No so: the man was 'severely reprimanded', and forced to sign a pledge that he would not repeat the offence.

There is no record of whether the defaulting nuns, willing or otherwise, were received back into the Order whose principles they had so grossly betrayed; the probability is that they made no attempt to return to the hard, ascetic if secure life they had been leading until then, having once tasted the pleasures of the outside world. One other brief item of interest connected with this small, out-of-the-way convent: Robert the Bruce's wife and daughter took refuge there during the campaign he was waging many hundreds of miles away to the north, and it was within the shelter of these walls that they heard the news of the triumph at Bannockburn.

Time, however, has dealt somewhat cruelly with the older parts of this hill-top town. Of his 'Shaston' (and the old name he used is still to be seen on the older milestones) Thomas Hardy was to write, a century ago: 'Vague imaginings of its Castle, its three mints, its magnificent

Gold Hill (from foot), Shaftesbury

apsidal Abbey, the chief glory of South Wessex, its twelve churches, its shrines, chantries and hospitals, all now ruthlessly swept away, throw the visitor even against his will into a pensive melancholy'. Not having known the town as it was, you may not feel as bitter about it as Hardy characteristically did; for though only the ruins of the nunnery, or abbey, remain visible today, there is still much to be seen and relished here.

For example, and perhaps most obviously, Gold Hill. This is a sickle-like curved street of large, uneven cobblestones that climbs from the valley to the highest point of the town. It offers a challenge to the feet, enabling you to appreciate the true feel of what it must have been like to walk the streets of medieval towns. It is no through-way. You can climb it by car (if your clutch and brakes are reliable and your load not too great), but at the top there is no exit, and you must do an elaborate piece of manoeuvring before your bonnet faces back down the way you have come and you begin the uncomfortable and potentially dangerous descent. Climbing, you have a high stone wall towering above you on your left, buttressing the old buildings that are barely visible from the cobbled way; on your right, each small house is stepped above the one below it and steadies the one above it with a massive necessary shoulder.

At the top of the hill, where you pause for breath and manoeuvre your car for the descent, there is a small museum. Stand with your back to it for a moment or two and take in the superb vista out and over the valley to the hills and downland reaching to the horizon. Glimpses may be caught between the alternating roofs of tile or thatch, and an even more spacious view from a point part way down the hill. Ironically, Gold Hill is the setting for one example of contemporary television advertising for a certain brand of loaf; the boy who struggles up it with his baker's bicycle deserves every penny-piece he may have been given by the promoters.

The museum is primarily of local interest, demonstrating the various activities that once went on in this small town with a long history. Among its exhibits is a collection of buttons representing a long and sustained period during which this was Shaston's sole industry, and a cottage industry at that. But the museum is interesting in itself as a building, even though unpretentious. For many years it was used by drovers bringing their cattle to the town's once busy cattle market. It was used also by vagrants wandering across the county with no fixed abode and ever on the watch for free bed and board, the 'sturdy rogues and vagabonds' of yesterday.

Close by is St Peter's Church, whose 13th-century tower rises splendidly above the upper end of Gold Hill. Only the tower dates back seven centuries, for the main fabric is largely of the fifteenth century, though it has a Tudor porch and the oak-timbered nave and chancel roof date from a century earlier. The crypt—so often the oldest surviving portion of an ancient church—was for a long time utilised as a beer-cellar by the landlord of a neighbouring public house! Fears have been entertained for the safety of St Peters', as it stands so close to the side of Gold Hill and it is by no means certain that those great buttressing walls can indefinitely withstand the outward thrust of the massive tower and nave.

Like Sherborne, Shaftesbury is essentially a town to explore on foot, even though this can make quite a demand on your stamina. So much that once existed, as Hardy lamented, has been swept away with the passage of time and man's apathy, yet it still contains much of interest on an unpretentious scale. There are few if any buildings of real intrinsic beauty, but many possess an aura of historic association. For instance, there is the old Fire Engine House, standing at the junction of Bell

Street and High Street. Here you may see the sort of equipment that was in use in the eighteenth century and later, when there was much more thatch about in towns than there is today. Old-style ladders and, notably, the long-handled fire-hooks that were necessary for the swift removal of burning thatch if a whole building and adjacent ones were not to be consumed by flames. Elsewhere there is Ox House, originally 'Mr Grove's House' and, in the mid-nineteenth century, called Ox Public House; you will find it mentioned in Hardy's last novel, *Jude the Obscure*.

In the stepped terrace of houses climbing uncomfortably up the curve of Gold Hill is the oddly named Blind House, mentioned in the town's records as early as 1476 and almost certainly used for a while as a gaol. Higher up, towards the top, is the Town Hall, with the old Court Room close by where the Quarter Sessions were regularly held until only a century and a half ago. It is here that you will find perhaps the most interesting exhibit-with-a-story that Shaston has to offer. Among the archives, the Borough Charters, the old Water Deed, the Silver Seal, the Borough Maces and the 'Standard Shaftesbury Bushel Measure' is the curious object known variously as the 'Besant' or 'Byzant'. It is certainly of medieval origin, and one might be inclined to think, because of its phallus-like appearance, that its origin is rooted in a much earlier period still, such as that of the Giant of Cerne.

Being a hill-top town, Shaftesbury had its water problems from the start. The nearest reliable supply was in the low-lying outskirts of the township at Enmore Green. For centuries, all the water used by the households inhabiting the upper and main part of the town had to be carried in buckets up one or other of the very steep hills leading to it. Certain families had a tradition of providing sturdy men who earned their living as water carriers, generation after generation. The strongest among them would push handcarts or buckets balanced, coolie-fashion, at opposite ends of a pole bent over their shoulders; or again, a less sturdy individual, even a woman in some cases, would carry a single oak-staved or possibly leathern bucket on the end of a short length of rope over one shoulder. Their charge ran at two pence per bucket and, so far as the carriers were concerned, the price payable was small.

In due course the water supply became the property of a succession of Lords-of-the-Manor; some kind of arrangement had then to be established between the fortunate landowner and the needy townsfolk. It is at the point that the Byzant comes into the story, though details of its origin are not entirely clear. Ornate, and indeed of very considerable value, it consists of a 'Prize Besom', or old-style broom such as gardeners use for sweeping up leaves. It became an integral feature of an annual rite carried out with some elaboration on the Sunday following Holy Cross Day, with associated dancing and May Day games held at Enmore Green, beyond the foot of Tout Hill, the source of that vital commodity. It became the link maintained between the owner of that water and the townsfolk who, in semi-feudal style, lived beneath his overlordship. Not until 1830 was water pumped and piped up to the town as a whole, when machinery at last made this a feasible proposition.

Tout Hill, already mentioned in passing, is so steep that in the days of the stage coach four additional trace-horses had to be harnessed to the four-in-hand teams to haul the coach and its load of passengers inside and out and freight from the bottom to the top. It was up and down this formidable approach-road that the long-distance coach ran between Devonport and London. It was scheduled to stop in the yard of the *Grosvenor Inn* daily, at 6.30 in the morning, when the exhausted shaft-horses and leaders (on the east-bound run) were changed for a fresh team and the auxiliaries were led back to their stables at the foot of the hill. It is in this long-established posting-house that there may be seen the famous Chevy Chase Sideboard, carved long ago in a most elaborate fashion from a single massive slab of oak; it depicts scenes from the famous ballad after which it was named. Tout Hill remains to this day a formidable challenge to traffic. No less a man than the great road engineer Thomas Telford himself was called in to see what could be done to regrade the hill. Its surface is better today than it used to be, but there was little that he could do to make the gradient easier, in view of the lie of the land.

5. Blandford, Wimborne, Wareham, Bridport and Beaminster

SHOULD THE CONTRAST between the grey Portland stone of Dorchester and the golden Ham Hill stone of Sherborne impress itself upon you, then once again you will find a very strong contrast between the three townships already considered and the next in line. Now the contrast is essentially that in building materials. The grey stone and occasional half-timbering of Shaftesbury is in complete, almost violent, contrast with that of Blandford Forum, a comparatively new town in which the Georgian style, in both materials and architecture, almost wholly predominates. Save for a very few specimens dating from an older period, almost all is in red, or sometimes russet-mauve, brick, with white stone quoins and much good use of pale yellow or cream plasterwork.

Why the word 'new'? Quite simply because the town *is* new. Though records show that there was a township on this river site (the '-ford' is a reminder of this) as long ago as the early thirteenth century, a Saturday market being held here from 1225 onwards, almost the whole of the original town was gutted by fire in the early part of the eighteenth century. Some 400 houses were destroyed and fewer than forty escaped. The fire broke out at two o'clock in the afternoon of 4th June, 1731, in a tallow-chandler's premises—always a potential source of disaster because of the stores of the raw commodity as well as of the finished product in the form of rush-lights and candles. Almost every one of the houses in those days would have been of timber framing in-filled with rough brickwork in the case of the more substantial ones and with wattle-and-daub in the much larger number of small ones. Most of the houses would have been roofed with thatch. The tallow-chandler's premises happened to be on the north side of the market place, and unfortunately the wind was blowing from that direction; the effect, as can be imagined, was catastrophic.

The fire spread so rapidly and with such fury that in no time at all the town's three man-handled fire-engines were engulfed and put out of action. Blazing thatch was sucked off the roofs and carried across the Stour to set fire to cottages and farms beyond the south bank. A lurid account of the matter in which the fire developed was recorded at the

time by the Reverend Malachi Blake. 'The church steeple took fire, and
that more than once,' he wrote. 'But by the great care and diligence of
some persons it was quenched again. However, about twelve of the
clock at night the fire was seen again in the middle of the roof. This
might have been stopped at first, had they had the engines, or could
have got ladders and vessels to carry water; but these were all burned. It
was towards two of the morning before it broke through the roof into
flame. Then the fire roared dreadfully, the lead melted, the stones split
and flew; nay, so fervent and irresistible was the heat that the bells dis-
solved and ran down in streams.'

Blandford, however, was fortunate in at least two respects. The then
Archbishop of Canterbury, William Blake, was a Blandford man, and
he at once subscribed a handsome sum of money for restoration work
to be begun without delay, at the same time using his wide influence to

Corn Exchange & Parish Church, Blandford Forum

obtain large sums from other sources. His influence was felt in the unlikeliest quarters. The Drury Lane Theatre Management 'resolved to have a play for the benefit of the unhappy sufferers from the late Fire in Blandford'. Money began to pour in almost as irresistibly as the fire had swept through the town; various town and city corporations, university authorities, churches large and small throughout the land, nobles, lords of manors and petty commoners alike all sprang to the relief of the stricken market town. There have been few examples in all social history of such widespread and practical expressions of sympathy, prior to our own times and tragedies such as that of Aberfan.

Secondly, Blandford was fortunate in having two architects, the brothers John and William Bastard. Like Sir Christopher Wren after the Great Fire of London in 1666, they set to work to redesign and rebuild the town. Within thirty years they had almost completed their work. It is almost entirely due to them, to their own inspiration and their ability to inspire those who worked with and for them, that Blandford today gives such a remarkable impression of unity, of complete integration. It has rightly been dubbed the most uniformly handsome Georgian red-brick-and-stone-built town in the whole of the south of

England. You may prefer the grey stone of Dorchester, and will almost certainly remember with greater aesthetic pleasure the golden stone of Sherborne; but you will not be able to deny the satisfying, if gentle, impact that Blandford makes upon the eye.

The Bastards' work is on every hand. They designed and built the impressive Town Hall, which stands next to the important Corn Exchange. They built the Parish Church, the destruction of which was so vividly described by the Reverend Malachi Blake; on a portico near by, designed in classical style, there is an inscription commemorating 'God's Dreadful Visitation by Fire'. They designed the beautifully proportioned house, known today as Electric House though it was built for their own use. It overlooks the market place and the Parish Church, against the wall of which stands the little portico in Doric style which they built to house the town pump. One of the finest houses that they were responsible for is Coupar House in Church Lane, a town house conceived in the grand manner. It has unhappily been marred by the insertion of a very obvious Victorian-style main door, and is now occupied by the local branch of the British Legion.

If you care to go in search of them, you can find a handful of houses that were built before the great fire of 1731 and, miraculously, survived it. One of these is The Old House, in The Close immediately to the north-east of the church; it was occupied by the medical practitioner in the actual year of the fire, and continued to be occupied by him while the rebuilding went on all about him. It is in striking contrast with the majority of the buildings, for it was designed in Renaissance style, with a steeply pitched roof and huge eaves that belong to an older period. Another building that survived the fire is the George Ryves Almshouses, in Salisbury Street; they bear the date 1682, so that they had only half a century of occupation before their inmates were confronted with almost certain disaster. God, they must have said in their piety, had been merciful to them. He was merciful also to the owner-occupiers of neighbouring Dale House, built just seven years later. In its garden is to be found a truly magnificent tulip tree, surpassed in this country, so far as can be established, only by the fine specimen in Kew Gardens.

The oldest building to have survived that fire, however, dates from very much earlier than either Dale House or Ryves Almshouses, though it is not wholly of its age. This is St Leonard's Chapel, originally a hospital for lepers but for generations past no more than a farmhouse barn. The enthusiastic connoisseur of buildings, or indeed the merely curious, may well feel it worth his while to look for it, to the east of the so-called Railway Arches, for it exhibits, if in confused and dilapidated form, a

variety of period styles. Parts of its walls almost certainly date from the fourteenth century; they contain ashlar and flint, rustic cob and plaster-work, three different varieties of stone, none of them of outstanding character, and brickwork of the same number of varieties as the Heinz products! There is some weatherboarding, too, which is acceptable; what is impossible, however, to accept, though one now has no alternative, is the rusted corrugated-iron that forms its roof. Do not allow this survival from pre-fire Blandford Forum to be your final impression of this charming Georgian town.

Blandford *Forum*, you notice. That is the name, clearly shown on the map and stoutly adhered to by its inhabitants. It suggests an origin dating surely from the Roman occupation of Wessex? But this is a fallacy. Blandford has been a market town of some importance for many centuries, and remains so to this day. It was originally *Chipping* Blandford, and that word, as we have already seen, invariably denoted the selling or bartering of marketable products. At some date not authoritatively established, through the snobbery of someone who may have been the abbot of a neighbouring monastery, it was decided that there was more 'class' in the Roman word *forum* than in the good old Saxon word *ceapping*; thus Blandford Forum it became, and remains to this day. It is the only town in all England that bears this dubious distinction. Not surprisingly, when Hardy was looking for a suitable name for the town, he retained the Forum, though he replaced the Blandford by Shottsford, the form which it takes in the map in each of his novels.

Some ten miles to the south-east, in the ever-widening valley of the Stour, lies Wimborne Minster. Like Blandford, the township is ordinarily deprived of its distinguished suffix, Minster. This is certainly to be regretted, for the great glory of the place is indeed its minster; its focal point and most memorable feature.

Like Shaftesbury, Wimborne is ancient. Indeed, the Romans established a base on this site nineteen centuries ago, for it was well watered and easy of access to and from one of their many beach-heads, the one we know now as Poole Harbour, barely five miles to the south. After their departure, the Saxons moved in, and Wimborne's proximity to the harbour became a considerable disadvantage, for the marauding Danes soon found it, recognised its usefulness and came ashore, moved northwards and swiftly set about ravaging what had by then become a Saxon township of some importance. Ethelred, King of the West Saxons and older brother of Alfred, who duly succeeded him, was slain in battle against the Danes on a site not yet authoritatively established; his remains were laid to rest, it is believed, within the grounds of a convent that had been established in 871 A.D. The convent, after its sacking, was rebuilt by Edward the Confessor, but designed now as a College of Secular Canons. Unlike most ecclesiastical and monastic establishments, it survived the Dissolution and was still occupied in the latter part of the sixteenth century.

Ethelred's remains now lie beneath a Purbeck marble slab which itself bears an effigy of the king-warrior; but this is actually dated in the fifteenth century, and it would be a bold man who would state categorically that the remains beneath the slab are truly those of the West Saxon king, in spite of the clear-cut inscription to that effect. Wimborne developed into a market town of importance, its economy deriving largely from the sale of wool from the vast flocks of sheep that grazed the thin turf of the downlands and the lusher turf of the Stour Valley. A school was founded 'to teach grammar to all comers'; it flourishes today as Queen Elizabeth's Grammar School, but its curriculum, as with all schools of ancient foundation, has now been very considerably widened in scope beyond that originally laid down by its founders. Doubtless it will shortly, like most if not all of our ancient grammar schools, be 'going comprehensive'.

Wimborne has been called 'a little cathedral city', and the title, if technically inaccurate, is at least poetically just. For the minster is emphatically its true centre. It is interesting, and indeed striking, from many points of view. Its exterior, for example, is a most unusual combination of white stone and chequered red; the centrally-placed one of its two towers rises splendidly above the main fabric, the lantern forming what looks like a crown. Until 1600 it carried a spire, but this collapsed. A contemporary record states that 'it was strangely cast down during a season of mist'. Taking its proportions as a whole, you may feel that the lantern-topped tower is more appropriate than a spire would have been. Parts of the fabric, including the tower, are of Norman origin, but the building as a whole was continued through succeeding centuries, much of it in the fourteenth and fifteenth.

Before you go inside the minster, glance upwards at the north face of the west tower. On it you will see what is known as a Quarter-Jack. It is a wooden manikin that strikes, as the term suggests, each quarter-hour. Being of wood rather than of metal, and exposed to wind and weather, the original Jack, carved and mounted in 1613, who then bore the resemblance of a monk, had in time to be replaced. From Napoleonic days at least he became a more martial than monastic figure; as you see him today he has the air perhaps of an old-time grenadier or fusilier.

The interior is a treasure-house, on a comparatively modest scale, of monuments and effigies and memorials of many kinds. Look for the Beaufort tomb, of 15th-century date. It bears two effigies beautifully sculptured in alabaster, a stone usually seen as snow-white but in this case of old-gold or honey-like hue, and all the more attractive for that reason. Look, too, for the Purbeck marble font, a remarkable example of the stone-sculptor's art in Norman times and therefore contemporaneous with the oldest portions of the minster as a whole.

Of even greater interest, perhaps, since tombs and effigies are to be found in almost every church in the land, whereas this feature is comparatively rare, is the Orrery, or astronomical clock. This dates from as early as about 1320, and is of particular interest because it shows not only the motion of the sun 'going around the earth'—as it was believed to do at the time of the clock's construction—but the motion of the

Wimborne Minster Quarter-Jack

moon round the earth as well. Another feature of unusual interest here is the Chained Library, to be found in the vestry. This dates from 1686, and was established 'for the free use of the citizens of Wimborne Minster'. Not surprisingly, the majority of the books are of a theological nature, but you will see there also a number of medieval documents, each bearing its appropriate seals, a 14th-century manuscript written and illustrated on vellum, churchwardens' accounts dating from 1403, and a volume of Sir Walter Ralegh's famous *History of the World*, so much of which was conceived and written, not in his gift-castle at Sherborne but during his long incarceration in the Tower of London after he had fallen into disfavour with Queen Elizabeth whom he had so well served and who was to treat him so harshly.

Close to the minster, on the east side, is the old Priest's House. Your immediate impression of it may well be that it is by no means old but, like so much of Blandford, dates from the Georgian era. Admittedly the front is Georgian, but this conceals a building that contains portions at least from many earlier periods, some dating back to the fourteenth century. Notable among these is one ceiling that was installed during the reign of Elizabeth I. The house is now a local museum and, as you would expect, contains exhibits that trace the long history of the little town from its very early days onwards. There is a sense of intimacy in this Priest's-House-turned-Museum that is wholly delightful; you can linger among the exhibits and savour what might be called the spirit of Wimborne Minster that has developed during its long history as a market town whose character survives to this day.

If you are pressed for time, you can take in the whole of this cathedral-town-in-miniature by viewing it, literally, 'in miniature'. For lying just off the road to the west is an exact replica of the town constructed to one-tenth scale. This means that the minster is some twelve feet in height, and the houses, shops, streets and other features all appear proportionate to this. There is the same pleasure to be derived from this bird's-eye view of Wimborne Minster as you may have found at similar sites in Bourton-on-the-Water, Ramsgate, and elsewhere; *Multum in Parvo* is the theme here. You may or may not relish the 'canned' music that emerges from the replica minster, but this, here as elsewhere, has become a tradition, and we have to accept it.

Because Wimborne lies so low you have to cross water from almost every approach. Indeed, there is a small hump-backed bridge in the very heart of the town, but here the one-way streets are so congested, being so narrow, that you have crossed it before you realise the fact. On the outskirts there are more pretentious bridges: one on the south spanning the Stour which is now flowing south-eastwards to its outlet beyond Christchurch and thus forming the natural border with Hampshire under the newly designated boundary, with arches that carry the road well above flood level on this low-lying terrain: Julian's Bridge, built in the mid-seventeenth century of darkish red sandstone but widened and overlaid with white stone in the next century and thus offering the same curious contrast in materials as strikes the eye when you look at the minster. There is, too, the long, narrow bridge on the west side, carrying the main road to Bridport, again built high so as to make passage possible when the broad-flowing Stour, augmented by the Allen, tends to flood the water-meadows. Of bridges such as these we shall be reading in the final chapter.

The township of Wareham is fortunate in a number of respects. To begin with, it does not lie on a through-route, as Dorchester does, and has therefore escaped the misfortunes that so often result from this position. Tourists tend to pass it by unless they have some specific reason for going to Poole or its harbour, which comes to within a couple of miles of it to the east. The town is on slightly rising ground, between two rivers, the Piddle (or Puddle, or Trent) and the Frome; this has given it a certain stature and importance from very early times, earlier even than that of the Romans. It is part-surrounded by the remains of an earthen bank, notably on its north side, constructed by Iron Age man. The Saxons reinforced this, though the township remained open, inevitably, on its south-eastern side and therefore fell victim to the marauding Danes as they made their way up the Stour Valley to Wimborne. But it survived, or recovered from, their depredations, as other Wessex towns were to do, thanks to the courage and determination of the natives of the area under the leadership of men like King Alfred and his successors.

It is on the northern earth ramparts that the small pre-Conquest Church of St Martin was built, in the year 1030, making it easily the oldest church in Dorset and among the very oldest in the whole country. It is true, and not surprising, that this Saxon church has had to undergo considerable restoration at intervals in the nine centuries that have passed over its head; but on the whole this has been carried out with imagination as well as skill and good taste.

The little church contains a strange contrast in basic features: the faint remains of wall-paintings that date back many centuries, if not to Saxon times; a masterpiece in sculpture carved in 1939 by Eric Kennington, whose seated statue of Hardy dominates Top o' Town in Dorchester. This statue, of T.E. Lawrence—'Lawrence of Arabia'—however, is a recumbent one; it lies in the north aisle, wearing the Arab costume which was so much beloved by Lawrence, that semi-legendary figure whose true qualities have perhaps not even yet been fully assessed either by those who revere his memory or by those on the other hand who have been doing their utmost to devalue it since his untimely death when he crashed on his powerful motor-cycle on his way to his cottage, Clouds Hill, six miles or so from Wareham to the west.

St Martin's of course is not Wareham's main church. This, the Church of Lady St Mary (an unusually worded dedication), stands on the site of what was formerly a priory, and its tower has been a landmark for shipping down the centuries. Parts of the church date back to the thirteenth century, but these are not too easy to locate, since very extensive restoration was carried out in the middle of last century. Some of its contents, however, are unmistakably old, and of very great interest. There is a hexagonal lead font dating from the twelfth century and virtually unique. It bears the effigies of the twelve apostles. Two effigies in Purbeck marble, carved in the thirteenth century, are also to be

Church and Priory House, Wareham

found in the church; they are knights, in full suits of armour beautifully fashioned down to the smallest detail. Another interesting feature, that links Wareham with Shaftesbury, is the marble coffin that once held the remains of Edward the Martyr, murdered on the orders of his jealous stepmother in Corfe Castle and subsequently transported for final burial in the hill town some twenty-five miles to the north.

Though this church as a whole gives impression of 19th-century restoration, it has its older portions. On a slightly lower level than the main fabric, on the south side of the chancel, there is a vaulted chapel that dates from medieval times; it is believed to stand exactly on the site of the chapel of the long-since-vanished priory from which, incidentally, the attractive Tudor house adjacent to it takes its name, Priory House of Lady St Mary.

Apart from these, there are few old buildings in Wareham for, like Dorchester and Blandford, the small town was swept by fire, and more than once. Much of its centre, therefore, consists of Georgian houses, few if any of them comparable with the work of the craftsmen-builders-architects John and William Bastard, though they possess a certain charm of their own. The Manor House, in South Street, is one of these, facing the bow-fronted windows of the *Black Bear*; another is The Alms-house, which survived the fire sufficiently well to be worth rebuilding on site in 1741, with the addition of a pediment and belfry. You will find it in East Street. Notice, by the way, these compass-point names; when Wareham was rebuilt, after a major fire in 1762, it was laid out largely in grid-fashion, after the Roman practice. This is paralleled in, for example, Chester to the north and Chichester to the east, though in each case they were Roman towns of very great importance whereas this Dorset township cannot make any comparable claims.

Thirty miles to the west of Wareham, by way of Dorchester itself or, if you prefer, along a sequence of coast and near-coastal roads skirting Dorset's South Downs, you come to Bridport. The name suggests a port, and a very long while ago this small township astride the valley of the Brit (why was this corrupted to 'Brid'? Something to do, perhaps, with the West Countryman's preference for the less harsh sound?) was in fact a port. The river estuary was wider and the sea inlet also. But this, unhappily for the Bridport men who made their living with ships in and out of the port, is the point at which the normal west-east movement of the shingle is in conflict with the east-west movement towards Lyme Regis. The stretch of water between East Cliff and West Cliff, now enclosing little West Bay, was unpredictable, often treacherous. Also, the Brit carried silt down to the shore line. One way and another, the original port ceased to be operable. Where the once-flourishing port was commercially busy, it is now largely the haunt of those who sail small boats and who are often based at the camp and caravan sites on the top of the cliffs which fall steeply towards the sea.

Bridport, with its notably broad main street, is largely Georgian in character. It exudes an air of spaciousness, of leisure, of prosperity. There are a number of reasons for this. It has been, for centuries, the place where cables and ropes were made for merchant ships and also vessels of the Royal Navy. Before through traffic developed to something like the proportions it has reached today, the pavements of many of the township's smaller streets, as well as those of the main street, were wider than the streets themselves. They were used as rope-walks, and indeed this use continued until very recent times. On these pavements simple but sturdy gear was installed for twisting the hemp. They were used also for drying-out the hemp, and the finished product. And since net-making went, and still to this day goes, with rope-making, the widest pavements and even the streets were much used for the making and drying-out of these nets. Increasing traffic has put an end to this, but the industry continues, mostly in the north-western district, though man-made fibres are nowadays more and more replacing the traditional hemp.

The town lies nearly two miles inland, out of sight and sound of the sea; but it comes close to being regarded as a seaport still. You cannot linger long in its wide main street, sloping eastwards up from the Brit and then gently downwards again before climbing up again to the South Downs four or five miles farther east. This throughway has something in common with, say, the main street of Marlborough; it offers the same sense of spaciousness. Midway along it on the south side is the impressive arcaded 18th-century Town Hall, notable for its balance of red brick and stone facings, built in 1785 by William Tyler, though the striking cupola was added to it at a later date. Close beneath it, at a blind corner, a narrow road runs south, heading for the water at West Bay. Opposite the Town Hall is a shop standing on the site of an inn where, in 1651, Charles II, fleeing from his defeat at the Battle of Worcester, sought refuge, heavily disguised, awaiting transport across the Channel to a haven in France. He had been let down and, he feared, actually betrayed, by a fisherman from neighbouring Charmouth.

The area immediately surrounding Bridport on the landward side was formerly much used for the growing of flax, and much of the town's wealth in years gone by derived from the processing of this locally-grown flax in the mills clustering alongside the Brit, whose waters flowed strongly down from the hills encircling Beaminster, five miles to

Main Street and Town Hall, Bridport

the north, and turned a number of water-wheels. All in all, this was a snug, self-contained little town, whose merchants and other successful inhabitants did themselves well. Granville House, Grove house and, most notably, Downe Hall, built in 1789 in grand style with a pilastered front of Portland stone, are some examples of the outward evidence of the prosperity enjoyed by these 18th-century industrialists and merchants; there are others, too, notably in East Street.

A number of these apparently 18-century buildings, however, consist of façades added to the original frontages of much older houses. Some people may regret this; but the fact remains that, owing to its prosperity, Bridport acquired something of the distinction of Georgian uniformity that is so immediately apparent in Blandford Forum. Nor did the town have to undergo the horrors of a major fire, as Blandford did, to achieve its present appearance. Fate may have been unkind in, so to speak, removing its immediate port facilities, by the unpredictable but inexorable movement of coastal waters; but at the same time it spared the town the catastrophic effects of that other and infinitely more destructive element.

Bridport lies at the lower end of a river that has its source five or six

93

meandering miles to the north in the horseshoe of downland that almost enclosed Beaminster (pronounced, if you wish to be immediately understood in the county as a whole and particularly in the western area, 'Be'mi'ster', or even 'Bemster'). Though little more than one-third the size of Sherborne, it is strongly reminiscent of that town, fifteen miles to the north-east, for it is largely built of that same glorious honey-coloured stone from the Ham Hill quarries. There are those who would maintain that, though smaller—and in part even for that reason—than Sherborne, Beaminster is every whit as beautiful. I go to one, and I go to the other; and I come away still not quite sure in my mind as to what I feel in that respect. Perhaps I may escape a final judgment by quoting William Barnes? He did not commit himself; but he wrote a small fragment, a characteristic couplet, that contains the vital epithet:

> *Sweet Be'mi'ster that bist a-bound*
> *By green an' woody hills all round.*

We can safely leave it to a true man of Dorset to express what he felt, and so what we too are almost sure to feel.

With the possible exception of Shaftesbury, standing proudly on its 700-foot escarpment, Beaminster must be the most perfectly sited of all Dorset's towns. East, west and north of it high downland forms a horseshoe of gently rounded hills, with much woodland as a kindly bonus punctuating their smooth outlines, filling in the hollows, offering tacit shelter to the township beneath them. To the north-east, Toller Down rises to over 600 feet, and it is on its lower slopes that the stripling Brit makes its first appearance. To the west, Clan Hill tops the 500-feet mark, and to the north Beaminster Down itself tops the 800-foot mark. There are not many hill tops in Dorset that surpass that impressive figure, though Bulbarrow does so by another hundred feet. For all that, Beaminster is best approached from the south, preferably along the minor road that follows the Brit closely along its west bank, climbing gently all the way.

The dominant feature here is the splendid tower of its Church of St Mary in the south-western outskirts. It is built of that same Ham Hill stone that characterises Sherborne Abbey. The tower is outstanding among those of Dorset churches in general, for it is comparable in stature and in ornamentation with those that lie on the other side of the Somerset border, which is only four miles distant. Somerset, of course,

Bulbarrow Hill, from Shaftesbury

is famous (like Suffolk) for the magnificence of the towers of even its minor churches.

Perhaps something of that tradition seeped across the border when this church was being built, early in the sixteenth century. Certainly there is no other church tower in the country which can truly be compared with it. Its many pinnacles rank with those of the Somerset churches at their best, and the exterior stonework is decorated with a multiplicity of stone-carved figures, particularly, as so often, over the west door and both on and between the buttresses. Some of these are so high above ground level that they can only be appreciated in their finer detail with the aid of a pair of binoculars. This is frequently the case with these ornamented church towers, and examples on an altogether humbler scale may be found in the gargoyles of many of Dorset's little churches, often in hamlets so small that you have passed through them almost before realising that you have done so.

Unfortunately the interior of Beaminster's church is very much less impressive than its exterior. A major job of restoration was carried through here in Victorian times—as so often, a bad period for this; the result again, though it may have satisfied those who commissioned the work, today can only be deplored. Few features remain that give pleasure to the eye of the beholder who looks for signs of age, if not of real antiquity, in such buildings. There is a pulpit that dates from the Jacobean era, and there are two quite impressive monuments to the Strodes of the mid-eighteenth century, whose family occupied the beautiful Tudor manor house to be found a mile or so to the south of the town. Somewhat surprisingly, both man and wife have been sculptured wearing Roman attire, for reasons never made clear. It was one of their ancestors, a benefactor to the town, who was responsible for the building of the almshouses, in 1603. Unusually, these stand almost within the precincts of the church, though, appropriately it may have been deemed by the founder, at a slightly lower level than the church itself.

Owing to the lie of the land, Beaminster is largely built on ground that slopes from north to south—like Sherborne. Apart from the church, its focal point is its square market place, overlooked by a number of 17th- and 18th-century houses that were built after a fire had destroyed much of the really old part of the town. Happily, the new buildings were constructed of Ham Hill stone rather than of bricks, so that they are more in keeping with the church, which wholly escaped the fire. Other buildings may be of brick so far as their main fabric is concerned, but they have mostly been faced with warm cream stucco and therefore, superficially at any rate, fit in with the overall impression of a golden stone-built town. It is not easy to believe that Beaminster was badly damaged by fire during the Civil War, when Royalist troops were installed in its many buildings. Hardly had the wartime experience begun to be forgotten when, in 1684 and again nearly a century later, fire again swept through much of the town and the humbler dwellings, those whose builders and owners had not been able to afford the luxury and comparative security of stone even though there were quarries so near at hand, were largely destroyed.

Quite apart from its striking appearance as you approach it from the south, or overlook it from some minor road or viewpoint to the northeast or north, Beaminster merits closer inspection. There are rewarding features at every turn. The mullioned windows of the *Eight Bells Inn* are a reminder of those that reach their apotheosis in the towns and villages of the Cotswolds; you will find the inn in Church Street, at the opposite end from the Strode Almshouses. Devonia House and Elm House, though their façades are in 18th-century style, are built of this lovely stone; they stand in strong contrast to the red brick (happily comparatively rare in Beaminster) of a house in Fleet Street named Burton End. With Farr's House, in Whitcombe Road, you are back again once more with the rich golden stone that characterises so much of this charming little town, whether it is on the noble scale of St Mary's Church or the more modest buildings such as proliferate even in the minor streets. Indeed, there is a sense of unity about Beaminster that has an immediate and enduring appeal; it satisfies the eye, but produces also an even deeper satisfaction that is perhaps less easy to define or even describe.

6. Villages and Hamlets

WITH SWEET BE'MI'STER we leave the category of small towns. Possibly Gillingham, in the extreme northern tip of the county, should have been mentioned, but it is not typical of Dorset, not as picturesque even as perhaps it once was since a rash of light industries spread through and about it. It does contain a handful of pleasant Georgian houses, and a church whose chancel dates back to the fourteenth century; there is, too, an endearing 17th-century twin monument to the Jessops, priest and physician, lying hand in hand in the vestry. But there is not much more than that.

Small as this county is, I do not think it is an exaggeration to state that no other in all England, even though very much larger, contains as many, let alone more, place-names that immediately arouse curiosity. Take a pin and, blindfold, drop it anywhere at random, and you will find that its point lies on or very close to some village, hamlet or even smaller cluster of habitations with a name that alone makes it worth searching out, even if it contains nothing of any antiquarian or faintly historic interest, not even a tumbled churchyard, a small thatched inn, a pair of stocks or a once-thriving smithy.

The odd, provocative names proliferate all over the map, if the scale is large enough to include them. They may be odd, or peculiarly musical, or suggestive of you do not know what; but they are there to stimulate the imagination. Purse Caundle and Bishop's Stourton, for instance; Child Okeford and Okeford Fitzpaine; Sutton Poyntz, Fifehead Magdalen and Fifehead Neville; Toller Fratrum and Toller Porcorum (did one Brother Toller have a brother who bred pigs?); Beer Hackett and Long Burton, suggesting the sustained enjoyment of England's traditional beverage, even if it is not the rough cider or 'scrumpy' of Somerset.

What is one to make of Ryme Intrinseca and the equally musical-sounding Iwerne Courtney and Hazelbury Bryan and Wynford Eagle? What of Goathill, Gussage St Michael and Gussage St Andrew, Langton Herring and Sixpenny Handley, Winterborne Came and Wool?

What of ecclesiastical-sounding Whitchurch Canonicorum, aristoc-
ratic-sounding Lytchett Matravers and mysterious-sounding Hammoon? And what, perhaps above all, of three names on arms of one
small signpost in the valley of the Piddle (or Trent): Folly, Mappowder
and Plush? All these names could easily be matched by others still
within the confines of this small county for their thought-provoking
qualities of sound, or sense, or both. Let us look at some of them, in no
particular order.

The transition between township and village must be made arbitrar-
ily, for the distinction has never been clearly laid down. One standard
dictionary defines a village as having 'from a few hundred inhabitants
to a few thousand', so we will make the transition by way of Sturminster
Newton. It lies in the upper reaches of the valley of the Stour, from
which, like so many smaller places, it takes its name. It still has a weekly
market, and is visibly expanding, so that before long it will almost certainly have moved into the larger category. So far as its centre is concerned, it has a number of buildings in a variety of styles, including
stone from the near by Marnhull quarries, cream-washed cob, some
half-timbering and some brick, and a good deal of thatch, though the
modern fabricated tile is more and more in evidence.

By the river side, half a mile from the centre of the village-township is
the 17th-century watermill. Indeed, the outskirts of Sturminster, which
has held a market for many centuries, lie amid green pastures at the
southern end of Blackmoor Vale, which Hardy used to refer to as 'the
vale of little dairies'. It may have been so in his day; but nowadays the
milk is of course collected in churns and tankers and delivered in bulk to
processing plants. Cows, rather than the sheep of the downland, are the
livestock mostly to be seen in this region.

Sturminster has one modest claim to literary association in that William Barnes was born here and went to the small school close by the
church that is to be found a little to the north of the cosy square.
Though the Church of St Mary underwent much rebuilding, notably
during the last century, it still possesses a fine wagon roof that dates
from the fifteenth century, complete with bosses and rose-centered stars
lovingly carved by true craftsmen. The eagle lectern was presented to
the church as a memorial to Barnes, 'late of this parish'. It is perhaps not
generally known that Hardy lived for a while in a stone-built house
close to the river that belonged to a long-forgotten dialect poet while he
was writing *The Return of the Native*. Why did he choose to write a
book in which Egdon Heath, the great area of wasteland so far to the
south, and west of Wareham, plays so significant a part, in a place so far

Sutton Poyntz

removed from it? Was it that he perhaps felt he could get it into truer perspective if he regarded and interpreted it from twenty miles or so distant?

Where shall we look next? At Bradford Abbas, perhaps, three or four miles to the south-west of Sherborne and, perhaps because of its proximity to that town and to the Ham Hill quarries not far over the border in Somerset, built largely of this glorious golden stone. It lies in the broad and shallow valley of the Yeo—a Devon name by association but belonging truly enough to Dorset even though it gives its name to Yeovil in the neighbouring county a couple of miles to the west.

The best approach to Bradford Abbas, again, is from the south, over a hump-backed bridge that dates from the late sixteenth century. The fine tower of its Church of St Mary the Virgin will have caught your eye long before you enter the single street of this compact little hamlet.

102

Almost the whole of the church dates from the fifteenth century, though there may well have been a sacred building on this site more than five centuries earlier. It is certainly the case that there was a rectangular apse here in the twelfth century, enlarged two or three hundred years later to give its present proportions. The impact of the small church as a whole, from whatever angle, is enhanced by the fact that the whole of it stands on a turf 'plinth' that is at shoulder level above the narrow road that part-encircles it, and you must ascend from this by a flight of stone steps to enter the churchyard.

A cluster of venerable yew trees cast a shadow over the western end of the church and the lower stage of the very impressive tower. It almost completely hides from view the remains of a medieval cross shaft that stands on a double-stepped plinth. The cross head is missing, but the octagonal shaft carries on two of its faces the weatherworn figures of the Virgin Mary and that of a man, possibly St John the Baptist. For the photographer, who instinctively makes for the west door of any church after looking at the south porch, this is frustrating. And particularly so in this case, where the doorway is of quite outstanding interest and beauty.

This west tower is strongly reminiscent of the Somerset-type towers, possibly because, like Beaminster, the place is so close to the border; it

Dairy Farming Country, Stour Valley

Bradford Abbas Church: West Door

is, however, much smaller than that of Beaminster. Its most conspicu-
ous feature is the display of eleven canopied niches, exquisitely carved
and flanked by great octagonal buttresses on each corner. Nine of the
niches are empty, but if you cast your eye upwards to the top row you
will descry two in which there are seated figures, one of which holds a
book. No one can say for sure whether at one time all the eleven niches
(and why the odd number, anyway?) were occupied, but it is generally
supposed that they were. Perhaps in an earlier age of vandalism than
ours the carved figures from the lower niches on either side of the beautifully designed west door were removed for someone's private and per-
verse pleasure; the loss is ours. To see these at their best, it is necessary
to visit the church in the late afternoon or very early evening.

In strong contrast to the beauty of the shallow porch in the lower part
of the tower you will find, on the north-west angle-buttress, a number of
curious notches. Church records reveal that this wall was used in olden
times as—of all things—a Fives Court! It is believed that these notches
were cut by some of the fives-players to enable them to climb up the

Bradford Abbas Church: S-E Face

tower wall to retrieve balls that had bounded out of reach on to the roof. There is an entry in the churchwardens' accounts for the year 1825 that reads: 'Paid to John Custard for printing a board respecting the fives playing, 4/-'.

The interior is less immediately striking than the exterior, though it contains a Jacobean pulpit and a variety of bench-ends that are quite remarkable for such an out-of-the-way little church: birds and beasts, human figures, vines, hops and ivy are all represented, among other subjects; they are all the work of yet another of those anonymous 15th-century craftsmen who, like those who carved the misericords, took pleasure as well as pains in their work. The roof, too, merits an upward glance, for it has some excellent hammer-beams with carved angels bearing scrolls in their outstretched hands.

Before leaving the church, look down at your feet as you stand in the chancel. You will see there a slab of stone bearing an inscription that will put you in mind of the Duke of Monmouth's landing on the Cobb at Lyme Regis, some twenty miles to the south-west. It reads: 'Under this stone lies the body of William Harvy of Wyke in the County of Dorset, who died of the wounds he received in the service of King James II at Bridport in ye said county on the second of July 1685'. He was obviously one of the men sent post-haste to oppose the Pretender's attempt to rally supporters for his abortive march on London.

Wyke Farm, with its imposing tithe-barn, a mile or so to the east and just off the Sherborne road, is a moated manor house that was the property of the monks of Sherborne Abbey until the Dissolution in the first half of the sixteenth century. In fact, the whole of the village was owned by the abbots—hence, as usual, its name to this day. Apart from its general air of serenity there is not much else of special interest here, though it is believed that the old inn, close by the church, the *Rose & Crown*, was used as a rest-house in the fifteenth century for the Sherborne monks when they were ailing. Though it later became a malt-house, it possesses an outstandingly fine stone fireplace surround, topped by panelling to match.

One of the place-names listed at the beginning of this chapter that evokes speculation is Ryme Intrinseca. The hamlet is to be found three miles or so to the south of Bradford Abbas and west of the larger village of Yetminster, in the wide valley of the Yeo. It is worth visiting, if only to say that you have been to a place with so odd a name. I have yet to hear an authoritative explanation of the Latin-seeming second half of the name. Perhaps it was devised by some cleric with a modicum of learning, the sort of man who added Forum to Blandford in place of the Saxon 'Chipping'? The first half of the name has nothing to do with rhyme; the hamlet is on the edge of a slope, and the old word for this has also given us the word 'rim'; it is as simple as that. Place-names are very frequently purely descriptive of their settings.

There is not a great deal to see here, but there are a few relics of the 13th-century church that stood on the site of the 17th-century one, dedicated somewhat unusually to St Hypolite; there are also some medieval windows that have happily survived the Victorian 'improvements' that are so noticeable in the church at Bradford Abbas. Glass, after all, is the means of communication between the exterior sunlight and the potential gloom within, and the medieval builders of churches thought of this point in their ornamentation whereas the Victorians all too frequently overlooked it.

Three miles to the south of Ryme Intrinseca is the trio of closely-related hamlets that share among them the forename Melbury: Osmond (Hardy's King's Hintock), Sampford, and Bubb. There are other villages elsewhere in Dorset with the same forename, such as Melbury Abbas. This trio may be found, all within little more than a mile of one another, on the northern slope of the North Dorset Downs, beautifully sited. The first-named lies lower than the other two, with water passing through it. It is one of Dorset's characteristic stone-built hamlets, though the buildings are not earlier than the seventeenth century, apart from the church, portions of which date from two centuries earlier at least. You will find something there, too, which is really ancient: tucked away in the chancel there is a piece of stone most curiously carved so that you might take it to be a deformed toad caught up in foliage. It has been dated to the eleventh century, and the early part of the century at that, though no one can say just why so early an example of a rustic stonemason's craft should have found a place in a medieval wall. Almost certainly the toad-like creature is intended to represent Abraham's ram, caught in the thicket of the Bible story.

Melbury Sampford is in the main a curious juxtaposition of a Tudor manor house of some distinction, Melbury House, and the adjacent Church of St Mary. This, too, has suffered at the hands of the Victorians, and the manor house also has been added to at intervals over three centuries. The most striking feature of the whole complex is without question the hexagonal lantern tower, which dates from the first half of the sixteenth century.

The third member of the trio, Melbury Bubb, is the most attractive of the three, though likewise miniature in scope; indeed, it is hardly more than a little group of stone-built cottages, a farm, a manor house, and a church dedicated to St Mary. Its site, on the slope of Bubb Down Hill, enhances it. Though the church was largely rebuilt in the middle of last century the architect involved had the good sense to retain not only its 15th-century appearance but also much of its original material, including as much of the medieval stained glass as was feasible. Where it proved necessary to replace lost fragments of this, care was exercised to incorporate newer glass that did not contrast too strongly with the old.

The tower, happily, is the original 15th-century one, and even though repairs have had to be effected here and there, they have been carried out not too obtrusively. The frieze and shafts make it more elaborate than many of Dorset's smaller churches. Inside, you should examine with some care the stone font which, as so often proved to be the case, is very much older than even the oldest part of the main fabric. It is quite certainly pre-Conquest, and almost certainly genuine Anglo-Saxon. It has a quite extraordinary frieze of carved animals—a lion, a wolf, a stag, a horse and others; they are all apparently engaged in a wrestling-match, so closely are they interlocked one with the other.

You will notice, too, that all the animals are—upside-down! Two explanations for this unusual, possibly unique, feature have been advanced by theorists. The more mundane of these is that the stone-work was formerly part of a very elaborate cross, removed from its unnamed site centuries ago and installed here, incorporated with other stonework to form a font. More picturesque—and surely no less likely—is the suggestion that the upside-downness is deliberate, signify-ing the overthrow of violence by virtue, indicating in pictorial form for those who could not read 'that all cruelty shall cease through the influ-ence of Christ'. If so, then this strange 1,000-year-old carving bears a message for every one of us today.

Six miles or so to the south of the Melbury trio are the Tollers—Fratrum and Porcorum; more unexpected Latin. They could be made into a trio by the inclusion of Toller Whelme, three or four miles to the north-west, though there is little to see there.

Toller Fratrum lies so much off the beaten track that you really need a large-scale map to locate it, along a narrow lane to which there is no exit. The name suggests an ecclesiastical origin: monks, or Brothers (the more attractive term), forming some small community. You are not very far wrong if this is your guess. There was an isolated group of Knights Hospitallers of St John of Jerusalem settled here many centu-ries ago. They were under the jurisdiction of the abbot of Forde Abbey, whose Chapter House at any rate was built in the twelfth century though most of the existing building is of more recent date. Like its occu-pants, those of Toller Fratrum were ejected at the time of the Dissolu-tion. As in so many cases up and down the country, where the monastic buildings were either razed to the ground and their material used for the construction of entirely new, secular buildings, or were converted to pri-vate use, Toller Fratrum became a private mansion; the refectory was converted into stabling and other buildings into what is known today as Little Toller Farm.

The surviving buildings merit close inspection. There are arched Tudor windows; there are ornamental stone finials; and there are carved heraldic symbols that include a lion holding a shield inscribed with the Royal Arms, a chained monkey looking into a (non-reflecting) stone mirror, a winged griffin and, in nice contrast to the fabulous eagle-head lion with winged body, a carving of a small boy playing what appear to be bagpipes. Close to this old building there is, at first impact somewhat unfortunately, a small and obviously 19th-century church, dedicated to St Basil. Take a look inside, and you will find, inset above the little altar, a stone carving that portrays St Mary Magdalene washing Christ's feet. It has been established that it was carved as long ago as the middle of the eleventh century.

Toller Porcorum, a mile or so to the west in the valley, has, as you might well guess, a less distinguished origin. In Saxon times the name appeared as Swynestholtre—another 'portmanteau' word, this time indicating 'a wood beneath whose trees pigs could root about for beech-mast'. Some time, obviously after the Conquest, someone changed the name about, again with the misguided feeling that a Latinised variant was preferable. So, the swine in the 'holt', or wood, were given a higher status and the hamlet's occupants perhaps made to feel that they shared something of the status of their Knights Hospitallers neighbours. Eric Benfield's belief is that of 'Celtic memories glimpsed through Roman culture, added to by a love of verse brought there by the Norse conquerors of the Dark Ages; and then the influence of the many church establishments in medieval days'. Whether he is right or wrong in the first part of his explanation, his final comment is almost certainly true.

Even if this tiny place was originally a pig-breeding settlement (like the countless '-dens' in Kent), it has its own church, dedicated to St Peter. Its tower is mainly of 15th-century construction, but there are portions of 13th- and 14th-century work in the north wall. Once again, the Victorians laid their unimaginative hands on the main fabric, and its contents, and by no means to their advantage. But there is a very old

Saxon Font, Toller Fratrum

font that justifies the effort of seeking out this hamlet even if little else does. It has been stated that it was originally a Roman altar, and therefore at least seventeen hundred years old; it is more likely that it started life as the capital of some pillar forming part of a church or other ecclesiastical building abandoned and demolished after the Dissolution, when so much irretrievable damage was perpetrated throughout the whole country.

It is a fact that very often indeed a church that has all too obviously been rebuilt or at any rate restored by the Victorians will prove to contain some treasures that make it memorable. Such is the case at Wynford Eagle, a minute hamlet beautifully named and beautifully sited a mile or so to the south of the Tollers, with downland rising to more than 600 feet on either side of it. The Church of St Lawrence, emphatically Victorian in conception, contains a striking piece of sculpture representing two dragons confronting one another in violent combat. The craftsman responsible for it was working eight hundred years ago. It would be hard to find a more powerful contrast than the general appearance of this church and this small masterpiece in imaginatively carved stone.

Near by is Wynford Eagle House—and who would not be happy to be able to put such an address on his notepaper? It is a manor house built of Ham Hill stone, in itself a guarantee of beauty, but remarkable chiefly for the asymmetry of its two main gables. The central gable over the porch carries on its peak the symbol of 'The Honour of the Eagle', deriving from one Guillaume de Aquila, who came over with William of Normandy. His descendant, Gilbert de Aquila, was in residence there in 1227. But the building you see today belongs to the early part of the seventeenth century, when it was owned and occupied by the Sydenhams, who supported the Parliamentarians during the Civil War. Of two brothers who lived there, one became a physician highly respected because he was lavish in his administration of laudanum; the other became Governor of Weymouth—an odd title to come across in local administration in this country; it was doubtless the result of his loyalty to the Paliamentary party just at the right time.

South-west of Wynford Eagle and separated from it by the enormous mass of Eggardon Hill, which rises to more than 800 feet and is among the highest points on the Dorset Downs, topped by a prehistoric earthwork-ramparted camp, or hill fort, lies another valley village, Askerswell. Small, secluded, well clear of the main road and dominated by the folds of the rolling hills to the north, it seems to shun publicity; but it deserves a visit none the less. Though, like so many of these small churches, that of St Michael was partly rebuilt in the mid-nineteenth century, the tower dates from the early part of the fifteenth century and the church possesses a font earlier than that by two hundred years. It also has, rather curiously, one half of a brass-indented memorial slab dating from the very early fourteenth century, the other half of which is to be seen in another small village eight miles to the west and bearing a name out of all proportion to its stature: Whitchurch Canonicorum.

Small as it is, the village deserves a leisurely look around. For one reason, it lies in the heart of Marshwood Vale, through which, among other small streams, the Char meanders west and then south, to creep gently into the sea at the little resort suitably named Charmouth, or at any rate a mile or so seaward of this. The Vale is the heart of the Dorset agricultural scene. From here, the farmers will assure you, comes the finest butter, the richest milk, the creamiest cream; from here, too, come the famous Blue Vinny (? veined) cheese, and the unique 'Dorset Knobs'. It is in Marshwood Vale that some of the finest oaks in the south of England grow. Broad Oak is actually the name of a hamlet in the Vale, and the many half-timbered buildings in the area attest to the quality of the oaks that went to their making.

As usual, the focal point of the village is the church. Though you may feel that most books about individual counties tend to lay too much emphasis on their churches, it does remain a fact that they are almost always storehouses of unusual and interesting information. The Church of St Wite is certainly no exception; indeed, it is more than ordinarily interesting. For one thing, nobody has yet established whether the saint to whom it is dedicated is a he or a she. The name may be Saxon, or it could be Breton. The owner could have been martyred by the Danes or, along with St Boniface, in Germany in the mid-eight century. The unique factor is that the saint's bones were at some time placed in a leaden reliquary which was left unopened until as late as the nineteenth century, in fact in 1900. They were then transferred to a stone coffin with a lid of Purbeck marble. The lid is unique in that it was pierced with three oval orifices. Anyone having a diseased arm or leg can insert the limb through one of the holes in such a way that it comes in contact with the bones of the saint. It is said—though one never meets anybody who has actually done this, or even witnessed the act!—that a miraculous recovery follows. The whole idea is slightly macabre; but it is not wise, even in these sceptical days, to dismiss such phenomena out of hand—as witness the ever-mounting number of instances today of supra-normal occurrences, whether spoon-bending or of greater significance.

St Wite's coffin is housed in the north transept of a church, parts of

Thatched Cottages, Abbotsbury

which date back to the twelfth century though more of it dates only from the fifteenth. The tower is of 14th-century origin. There is a Jacobean pulpit, and a good deal of fine linenfold panelling and other oak carving, notably in the chancel, and some medieval stained glass. But it is of course the coffin of St Wite that is its proudest possession, its unique treasure. The mystery that surrounds this patron saint, of whatever sex, has made Whitchurch Canonicorum one of the small handful of 'holy places' on a miniature scale to be found in this country as a whole. It may not compare with Glastonbury in grandeur, or even with Walsingham in distant Norfolk; but for all that it remains a very special place of pilgrimage even today.

If there were space available it would be possible to continue to mention and describe the villages and hamlets at this end of Dorset almost indefinitely. But perhaps enough has been written already to make the point that there is interest as well as beauty at every turn, and often in the unlikeliest corners. It is time therefore to move eastwards across the county and see what there is to be found among those in that region. We can make the journey—it cannot in any case be a long one—either coastwise or over the South Dorset Downs. If we choose the former, then Abbotsbury offers a useful point of transition.

Abbotsbury is midway along the unique coastal feature, Chesil Bank, and at the westward end of the long, narrow lagoon that lies behind this

112

and is divided into West and East Fleet. The village is built almost
entirely of a stone richer in hue than that of the Purbeck quarries to the
east: warm, mellow, soft and perfectly married to the abundant thatch
so characteristic a feature of the county as a whole. The name it bears is
self-explanatory. Here in former times there was a Benedictine abbey.
Most of its buildings have long since fallen into ruin, but there remains
still the magnificent tithe-barn, a characteristic feature of so many of
these great foundations.

It is a mammoth building, not far short of 300 feet in length and over
thirty feet from wall to wall, with a splendid roof; it is buttressed, as
such buildings had to be in order to carry the roof, and especially when,
as here, they were exposed to the full force of prevailing winds. Though
the village itself lies half a mile inland from the sea shore, the abbey and

113

its associated barn stand on high ground, unsheltered from the west and south-west. The barn is a visual reminder of the old tradition, implicit in its designation, that moneys due to the abbot could be paid over in kind rather than in cash: one tenth of his income from every contributor, whether prosperous land-owner or humble peasant.

The village is probably even better known for its Swannery than for the remains of its abbey, impressive as these are. At the western end of the lagoon, beyond the slopes crowned by the ruins, there has been, as records show, for at least six centuries a permanent community of swans and cygnets, jealously protected. Their numbers have on occasion risen as high as 1,000, though normally there are not more than five or six hundred at any one time. Even that figure is impressive; nowhere else in the country can so many of these large and graceful birds be seen all at once. There are a number of other waterfowl, but it is the vast flotillas of swans that leave the indelible memory.

There is much else to be seen in the immediate neighbourhood of Abbotsbury. From the hill by which you descend to it from the west you can obtain a remarkable view of the whole scimitar-like sweep of Chesil Bank as far as Portland Bill; but you must have good, clear weather for

Abbotsbury Swannery

this, and unfortunately there nearly always seems to be a haze that blurs the outlines. Perhaps the only real solution is a shot from a helicopter on some day of clear, cold sunlight.

High on a hill top to the south-west stands St Catherine's Chapel, known locally as the Seamen's Chapel, perhaps because it offers an outstanding landmark for coastwise shipping, 250 feet above the water. It has one charming small feature, however, that may not be generally known: there is a space in one of its pillars into which, if you should happen to be on the look out for a spouse, you may drop a pin; your wish, if tradition is to be accepted, will be granted! The chapel, though small and wholly exposed to the prevailing south-westerlies, like the tithe-barn below is massively buttressed. This accounts for the fact that it has survived for no less than six hundred years. Being so remote, it is ordinarily kept locked, but the climb to the top of the hill, key in hand, is well worth your while, The chapel unexpectedly has an unusually ornate barrel-vaulted stone ceiling. The buttresses serve a dual purpose: they have enabled the building to resist the gales and have prevented its walls from being forced outwards by the sheer weight of this fine roof.

Even a cursory glance at the map reveals that in quite a small area between Abbotsbury and Blandford Forum there is a cluster of place-names all of which include the word Winterborne. The word refers to a certain type of stream, of which there are quite a number in the county, which vary in character more than most others do. Because of the nature of the soil and subsoil through which they flow, they have a tendency to degenerate into mere trickles of water, sometimes vanishing altogether, particularly during very dry spells. When the autumn rains begin they reappear, and can swell to quite considerable proportions. Chalk, like certain limestones, can bring this about. So, they are called winter bournes—winter streams—an easy generalisation.

Look about you in this region: Winterbornes Abbas, Steepleton, St Martin and Monkton; beyond Dorchester, Winterbornes Clenston, Houghton and Stickland, Whitchurch and Tomson, Kingston, Anderson and Zelstone; and other besides. All are very modest clusters of dwellings, with churches of lesser or greater interest at their heart, and often a manor house of particular interest somewhere close by.

Winterborne Clenston is one of these. Though the church is little more than a century old, the manor house of the de Winterbornes was originally built in 1230, though what you see of it today is basically fifteenth century, lovingly rehabilitated some twenty years ago. It offers what might be safely called a symphony in building stone: grey Portland, Purbeck marble, flint, slabstone roof tiles and mullioned windows of the richer Ham Hill stone; all have united to present an integrated and satisfying *ensemble*.

Close by is a huge and lofty barn, not comparable with that of the abbey already described, but impressive none the less. And especially from inside, for it has a hammer-beam roof that one would hardly have expected to find in such a building, but rather in the Great Hall of some ancient manor house itself. It is possible that this roof may have been dismantled, transported and re-erected here after the Dissolution of Milton Abbey three miles or so to the west.

Five miles cross-country to the south-east is Winterborne Zelstone, like its near neighbours Anderson and Tomson very much at the back-of-beyond. The Church of St Mary is unusual for its alternating bands of darkish stone and grey-white flint, while its squat tower is of Port-land stone, and crenellated. On the west side, easier to see than most gar-goyles because the tower is of so modest a height, is one that has the homely appearance of an ox. Winterbornes Anderson and Tomson are so diminutive that they appear only on the larger-scale maps. But then, this is one of the more endearing features of the county. The first-named unexpectedly has a manor house built in the early years of the seven-

Affpuddle Church

teenth century, and of a material unusual in a district where Purbeck and Portland stone generally prevail. It is built of brick, every third course of which is of darkish purple hue, the whole being topped by two impressive quartets of chimneys. Winterborne Tomson has no manor house, but its small church of grey stone and flint dates from the twelfth century, and from its site as well as its style offers a curious resemblance to a ship at anchor.

Though there are many of these winter bournes, there is a larger stream, or river, in this area: the Piddle. It appears also on the map as the Trent. It gives its name to a number of villages and hamlets that lie secluded in its wide and gently sloping valley: Piddlehinton, for example; and, with a change of vowel that is most frequently found in the

117

Affpuddle Tithe-Barn

lower part of this valley, Puddletown and Tolpuddle, Affpuddle, Turners Puddle and Bryants Puddle. Higher upstream than these there is a village that, so to speak, has hedged its bets: Piddletrenthide.

In the upper reaches, of course, the valley is narrower and rather steeper; the shoulders of the Downs rise to 500 and 600 feet or so, squeezing the river valley between them. Piddletrenthide spreads along it for something like a mile in all: warm-hued stone-built houses sprawling southwards from the 15th-century church, which possesses one of the finest towers to be found among the county's smaller churches, though it does not begin to compare with the one at Beaminster. The tower, and indeed most of the church, date from the fifteenth century, while the south porch dates from the twelfth, and is remarkable for the gargoyles above it. Here again, stone of varying hues is to be seen in striking contrast to the cold, hard flint that is to be found in such abundance, as always in regions with a chalk subsoil like neighbouring Hampshire and West and East Sussex; each is a foil to the other.

118

Tolpuddle

This same admixture of hewn and dressed stone and raw flint is to be seen in the church at Affpuddle, eight miles downstream. The building material has been set out in chequerboard fashion, and the whole is the more impressive for its back-drop of clustering yew trees with their green so nearly black. The exterior is less attractive than many of these churches, but there is something especially interesting within. The church is dedicated to St Lawrence, portions of it dating back to the early thirteenth century, though there was almost certainly a church of a kind on this site in the tenth century, when one Affrith donated 'a parcel of land' to the abbey of Cerne.

You will see on the chancel wall a memorial to one Edward Lawrence which bears the Lawrence coat-of-arms. Is there something familiar about this? Of course! you have seen it on the flag of the United State of America, commonly known as 'Old Glory'. The mother of George Washington was originally a Miss Lawrence, and her family's arms are quartered here with the Stars and Stripes. Ask any native of Affpuddle and he, and more particularly she, will assure you that this is true. Not far from the church is another tithe-barn, solid and smoothly thatched, presumably once the property of the abbey to which this 'parcel of land' was donated.

The best known of all the Piddle, or Puddle, towns is of course Tolpuddle, a mile to the north of Affpuddle and, unfortunately right on a main road. At close quarters it is not an attractive village, though seen across the low-lying fields it exudes charm, the main road being well out of sight; the story which, so to speak, put it on the map was told in the chapter in which Dorchester is described.

Before moving farther eastwards, into the area drained by the Stour, we should take a look at some of the engaging little hamlets that lie among the folds of the downland to the north-west and north-east of Piddletrenthide. The order is immaterial, for anyone wanting to get the feel of Dorset, particularly that of rolling downland, will soon realise that a large-scale map and a deliberately leisurely approach, almost without any specific objective, is the only right and proper one.

Take Plush, for instance: a hamlet so small that you must look for it with some care, and even determination. Whence the odd name? Plush, like Melplash in this same county of odd and intriguing place-names, is a variant of the Saxon *plaesc*, that suggests, with a hint of onomatopoeia, the movement of water in gentle mood. A little stream does in fact run quietly through this miniscule place. Standing on the steps of its *Brace of Pheasants* inn (where you may eat astonishingly well for so hidden a locality), you can just hear it above the song of the birds in the abundant trees. And you can hear, too, the quiet voices of men engaged in, you might well say, the unlikeliest of tasks: running an orchid-producing market garden.

Two or three miles to the north, over the lift of the downland on a northward-falling slope, lies Mappowder. It is not perhaps among Dorset's most beautiful villages, but it has certain claims to distinction. As with Plush, its name is good Saxon, originally *malpeldrea* and recognisably 'maple tree'; how the transition to its contemporary form came about is anybody's guess. Its Church of SS Peter and Paul dates back to medieval times and there is still some 15th-century glass in its windows; a cottage close to the churchyard was once the home of the forgotten novelist T.F. Powys, one of a family of gifted brothers of whom the best known in his day and for some time afterwards was John Cooper, author of the powerful work, *A Glastonbury Romance*.

More beautiful, and indeed of far greater interest than this trio of oddly-named hamlets is Cerne Abbas, five or six miles to the west and sited on its own small river, the Cerne, separated from the Piddle (or Trent) by high rolling downland that rises to more than 750 feet above sea level. As its name betokens, there was once an abbey here. It was a Benedictine abbey, founded in the late tenth century, that flourished until the time of the Dissolution. Inevitably, little of it remains to be seen today, for as so often much of its stonework was cannibalised by 16th-century and later builders who found it a valuable source of supply of ready-hewn stone. You do not have to be an expert to detect evidence of this malpractice in many parts of the village.

Such portions as do remain, however, are exceptionally fine. If you turn out of the main street into Abbey Street, leaving the *Royal Oak Inn* on your right and passing a row of medieval houses of your left, some of which almost certainly contain stonework from the ruined abbey, you come to the 15th-century Church of St Mary almost facing them and, immediately ahead of you, at the end of this short street, a handsome stone building, Abbey House.

Beside this and behind it, screened by a high stone wall, will be found the original Abbot's Hall, with an elaborately designed oriel window, an impressive relic of the great gateway through which the abbey precincts were entered, and part of the abbey guest house, an essential feature of every such establishment throughout the land. The tithe-barn, unlike the one at Abbotsbury, lies at the other end of the village and was partially converted in the eighteenth century into private dwellings. But it does date from the fourteenth century and still retains much of the dignity that characterised almost all these ancillary monastic foundations.

Dominating this village that once contained a Benedictine abbey and so much of which reminds the visitor of its monastic tradition and associations is the hill immediately to the north of it, appropriately known as Giant Hill. For it bears on its rounded summit, cut out of the chalk beneath the scant turf, the outline of a male figure 180 feet high, brandishing in his right hand a shillelagh-like club that must be a hundred feet long. Even more spectacular is his up-thrust male organ, symbol of virility at its most rampant, perhaps twenty feet in length. The outline and predominant feature have, since Victorian times (when in some households even grand-piano legs were swathed from view), been maintained clear-cut and challenging. The figure is almost certainly of Romano-British origin. Though certainly more spectacular, it is comparable with the chalk-cut figure known as the Long Man of Wilmington, on the South Downs of East Sussex. Equally certainly, even in this so-called enlightened age young men and girls have been known to clam-

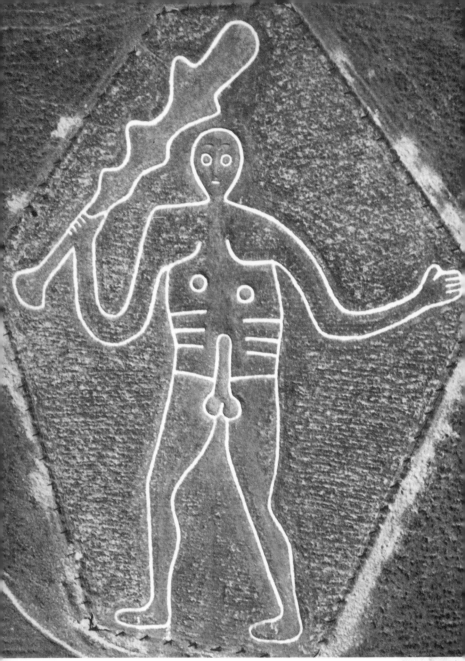

The Cerne Giant

Medieval Cottages, Cerne Abbas

ber up the steep turf slope and stand together on the relevant portion of
the Giant's anatomy, in silence, and with the deeply-felt conviction that
their love-making will in due time bear fruit. This pagan figure—some
refer to him as Hercules—sprawled provocatively on this hill top many
centuries before the Benedictine Order founded their abbey here in the
tenth century; and, unlike the abbey, it survives to this day.

It would be hard to find a greater contrast to Cerne Abbas than the village of Milton Abbas, eight or nine miles away across the hill tops. Far
from exuding an aura of antiquity, it strikes one immediately as being
almost 'brand new'; and in fact this is almost literally true. The Abbas
part of its name relates to the abbey founded in the tenth century as a
Benedictine monastery lying a bare half mile to the west and now, as an
abbey, long since derelict. Some two hundred years ago Lord Milton,
the 1st Earl of Dorchester, bought what remained of it and had a mansion built for himself that incorporated the 15th-century Abbot's Hall
with its magnificent hammer-beamed roof. It has since become a boys'
school. He did not, however, welcome the proximity of a number of
humble cottages that had over the years grown into a small hamlet cen-
tred on the abbey; he therefore had them razed to the ground, save for
one small, unobtrusive thatched building.

But he was not wholly blind to the needs of the occupants. Selecting a site sufficiently well removed from his mansion, he built for them what might be called an integrated village, certainly the first of its kind in the country. It has one single street, sloping gently between two rows of detached cottages, each separated from its neighbour by an identical tree, each with an apron of lawn slanting down to the road, each with a pair of chimneys protruding through its thick, cosy thatch. The only exceptions to these uniformly designed cottages are the inn, the almshouses of mingled (and not too happily) red brick and flint, and the small church of reddish stone.

The village gives the impression of being scrupulously cared for: every little apron-lawn is cut to the same depth; every bush and shrub, almost every flower and plant, conforms with that next door on either

124

side; every house is painted regularly, and in identical or closely matching colours; every window seems to have been polished inside and out every day. True or false, fact or fantasy, this is the impression given. After wandering about and lingering in so many antiquated and unconformably designed hamlets and villages, there is something just a little chilling, even on the sunniest of days, in the impact produced by Milton Abbas. Does every inhabitant have to take the same number of pints of milk every morning? Is there a curfew that decides the hour at which every one of them has to switch off the television and go to bed? Looking back on the various times that I have passed through (not lingered in) Milton Abbas, I do not recall ever having seen anyone gossiping at her door; perhaps that, too, is one of the conditions of tenancy.

Before completing this chapter on the villages and hamlets of Dorset it may be a good thing to turn back to some of those that are truly old and have not experienced what happened to Milton Abbas, which would seem to demonstrate the ultimate in ignoble snobbery.

There is a cluster of these not far away to the north-east, in the upper Stour Valley. Fifehead Magdalen, for example, and Fifehead Neville. The first-named is barely a mile from the Somerset border, its variegated houses (in such strong contrast to those just looked at) and its

Abbey Gateway, Cerne Abbas

The Royal Oak, Cerne Abbas

Milton Abbas

Church of St Mary Magdalene with its 13th-century tower almost surrounded by trees. This is dairy-farming country, and its neighbour, Fifehead Neville, a little lower down the valley, is set about with pastureland and water-meadows, hedge-bound fields and brooks that offer water-splashes at unexpected turns in the lane, so that it is unwise ever to drive at more than very leisurely speed.

Hammoon, on a tributary of the Stour to the east of Sturminster, is miniscule, but worth searching out by way of a winding lane that gives the impression of wishing above all else to lose itself as soon as possible. There is a beautiful though small manor house with an elaborate porch and gracious mullioned windows that dates from the sixteenth century. It lies at the end of a cul-de-sac, secreted by trees and an ornamental garden from the traffic-free lane so that you will miss it altogether if you do not know where to look for it. An elderly man trimming a hedge, possibly the owner, stepped out of the way, recommending the best vantage-point for a photograph; owner or not, he was obviously proud of this gem of a building, which is now a farmhouse.

At the point at which this cul-de-sac branches off the lane, there stands the towerless Church of St Mary, roofed, again not too happily, with red tiles. Small as it is, it merits a look inside. There is an odd assortment of church furniture: an early 17th-century pulpit; a 15th-century stone-carved reredos, said to have been salvaged from a scrap-dealer's yard (what a find!); and a beautiful oak door which almost certainly dates back to the year 1400. The name of this minute hamlet is, like so

Hammoon Manor House

many others, a corruption of a much older name. It was the manor of the famous dynasty of Norman barons, the de Mohuns; the name, quite simply, means the riverland home of the de Mohuns. The first de Mohun spelt his name 'de Moion'; with forty-seven Normans beneath his banner, he fought for William the Conqueror in 1066, and this was his reward.

Still on low-lying ground, close beneath the hills that rise, with Cranborne Chase to the east, is Fontmell Magna—not so large as its name suggests—just short of the Wiltshire border. Its setting, with Fontmell Brook and the small lake that it forms, is idyllic. So too is that of Iwerne Courtney (known also as Shroton, a much less melodious name), two miles to the south. At Fontmell there are some of the most attractive examples of ornamental thatch in all Dorset; we shall come to this aspect of the rural scene in the final chapter. In Iwerne Courtney flint and brick are satisfactorily 'married' with the more usual stone, and the hamlet is dominated by the 15th-century church tower. At one stage in the Civil War no fewer than three hundred local men were herded into the church and the doors barred against them. Their offence? A mutual pledge to resist all comers, whether Royalists or Roundheads, intent on spoliation. Cromwell's officers were more merciful than some other have been known to be; at least they did not set fire to the church and immolate the reluctant congregation. Incidentally, the hamlet lies at the foot of the 600-foot-high Hambledon Hill on which, a century later, Wolfe of Quebec trained his men in readiness to scale the Heights of Abraham.

There are a number of Iwernes, all within a short distance of one another. It is true that Iwerne Minster has no minster, but its Church of St Mary, parts of which date back to the twelfth century, possesses one of the very few spires in a county which, like Somerset to the west, goes in rather for castellated towers than tapering spires. Two miles to the south is Stepleton Iwerne, with Stepleton House as its dominant feature. It was built in the seventeenth century and greatly extended by the addition of two large wings in the following century. The relatively straight road south to Blandford here forms a pronounced horseshoe loop. The story, which may be apocryphal, is told that William Beckford's nephew resented the closeness of the road and its traffic and turned to his eccentric uncle, author of *Vathek* and creator of Fonthill, for help. Beckford took action in his lordly way. He dined the County Commissioner one evening and, when the man was very much in his cups, handed him a paper to sign. The paper was an order to have the main road blocked to the north and south and to be replaced by a loop to the west. The workmen moved in without delay, and the peace and seclusion of Stepleton House was assured; traffic has been incommoded by this loop ever since.

There are a number, too, of Tarrants: Crawford, Gunville, Hinton, Keynston, Launceston, Monkton, Rawston and Rushton—quite a bevy. Not one of them is outstandingly beautiful, at least compared with some of those farther to the west; but there is something picturesque or interesting, or both, in every one of them. The Greek cross-shaped Church of St Mary at Rushton, for instance, and the unusual carving round the 'squints'—in themselves a comparatively rare feature in churches such as these; Tarrant Crawford's church, of the same dedication, parts of which date from the twelfth and thirteenth centuries. Keynston's Church of All Saints, though it is little more than a hundred years old, is interesting outwardly at least because the stone of the tower has a positively greenish hue. And so on; you must seek them out for yourself. They all take their name from the little Tarrant, that flows out from Cranborne Chase to join the Stour on its way south-eastwards to the sea.

Flint-and-stone, Tarrant Keynston Church

Tarrant Keynston Church Tower

I look back over the map of Dorset and realise that, for every single village and hamlet mentioned in this chapter I could equally well have mentioned a number of others in detail, all of them just as deserving. No mention (as yet) of Spettisbury (though mention is to come), or Chaldon Herring, or Belchalwell or Batcombe—set so perfectly in a sort of amphitheatre—with the ancient stone pillar that probably dates from pre-Christian times, the stone on which Alec D'Urberville made Tess lay her hand while vowing never again to put temptation in his way. No mention of Long Bredy or Little Bredy, or Hinton Parva or even of its neighbour, Hinton Magna.

There is no end to the tally of tantalising place-names, but the temptation to delve further among them has, alas, to be resisted. I do so herewith, and embark on the final chapter, a gallimaufry of good things, as I hope you will agree; but loosely assembled, picked almost at random from Dorset's infinite variety as it were with a roving pin poised over my well-worn map.

7. Around and About

SMALL THOUGH IT MAY be in comparison with many other counties, Dorset has its quota of Great Houses. None of them can compare, in size, splendour or popularity, with those in the top league: Beaulieu, Blenheim, Woburn, Castle Howard, or neighbouring Longleat in Wiltshire and Montacute in Somerset. But that is not to suggest that they are not outstanding and memorable in their own right. Kingston Lacy, near Wimborne Minster (and few Great Houses anywhere in the country are more mellifluously named), dated from the seventeenth century. Its brick exterior was later dressed with stone in a more classical style, and the somewhat colder effect may not please everyone. But the two-mile-long avenue of beech trees lining the approach drive lends natural charm to the comparative austerity of the building at the end of it.

To the south-west of Kingston Lacy on the north side of the Purbeck Hills and close to the stretch of moorland that Hardy named Egdon Heath is Creech Grange. As its name implies, it was originally a granary, in fact the property of Bindon Abbey near by, which fell victim to the Dissolution. A house was built here in 1540 by the Lawrence family, who occupied it for a hundred and fifty years before selling it to the Bond family (whose name is commemorated in London's Bond Street). They enlarged and rebuilt the house over the years, laying out its ornamental park and incorporating much stonework from a Cluniac monastery that had been built on the slopes of Purbeck a few miles away and of course abandoned like all the others. The grey stone gives an impression of lack of warmth, but the gardens do much to compensate for this. The house is overlooked by a 'Folly' that stands high on Ridgeway Hill, its rugged stonework now blurred by the inexorable growth of rampaging ivy.

At the extreme opposite end of the county, so literally on the Somerset border that some map references locate it actually in that county, is Forde Abbey. With possibly one exception, this is the most beautiful and ancient of Dorset's Great Houses. It stands on the site of a Cistercian abbey that was founded as long ago as 1142, when it was designed

Creech Grange

to house no more than twelve monks. Parts of that early foundation still survive. The 12th-century Chapter House, for instance, that became the chapel, and the 13th-century *dorter*, or dormitory, which is remarkable for the fact that it is no less than 150 feet in length and possesses a fine, yet simply executed ceiling. After the Dissolution it fell into sad decay, but fortunately, instead of becoming a free-for-all quarry, it survived and was rehabilitated by one Edmund Prideaux, Cromwell's Attorney-General. It is he whom we have to thank for what we see here today, for he extended and beautified it with love and skill.

The main front of Forde Abbey is no less than 400 feet long, with a noble porticoed entrance-block and tower and castellated along its full length and richly windowed on ground, first and even second floor. In strong contrast with Creech Grange, the whole building is in the honey-hued stone from the Ham Hill quarries; with the sun in the south-west, it seems to exude an almost living golden glow.

It could, however, have been destroyed entirely and so lost to us for ever, for a successor to the first Prideaux was rash enough to throw in his lot with the Duke of Monmouth when he landed at Lyme Regis, seven miles to the south, in 1685. His life, and Forde Abbey, were spared; but he had to pay a penalty of no less than £15,000—a truly enormous sum in those days, equivalent in terms of millions today. The façade looks out over greensward, with a water-lily-strewn lake in the immediate foreground and trees beyond. Behind that façade, in addition to the many great rooms hung with tapestries made by weavers from Brussels and representing the Acts of the Apostles, brought to England by Charles I, there is the famous Monks' Walk, stone-flagged, whitewashed, with deep window embrasures and clean-cut vaulted ceiling, the original dormitory and quite possibly the most memorable feature of the interior, not in spite of so much as because of its simplicity, its evocative austerity.

Five miles to the north-east of Dorchester, in the valley of the Piddle and midway between Puddletown (the 'Weatherbury' of Hardy's *Far From the Madding Crowd*) and Tolpuddle, of the Martyrs' fame, there is to be found, surely the pearl among the county's Great Houses, Athelhampton House. There has been a dwelling on this site for eight hundred years, but the larger part of what you see today was built about 1470, with minor additions in following years. There are connoisseurs of such buildings who maintain that it is the finest medieval stone-built manor house, not merely in Dorset but in all England.

It seems to have just everything, save magnificence in sheer size. You pass through a gateway in a massive boundary-wall and find yourself immediately confronting, beyond lawns and a gravel path, an L-shaped building, battlemented save for its two small and one large gable, two-storeyed along one arm of the 'L' and three-storeyed along the other. It has a steeply pitched roof through which a pair of beautifully proportioned dormer windows boldly project, each with its graceful finial and backed by contrasting chimney-stacks. The fact that it is L-shaped gives a curious impression of welcome; and since the house has been occupied throughout its five long centuries of existence in its present form, you become instantly aware of this as a 'lived-in' home as you cross the threshold. This is especially the case if you are fortunate enough to have visited Athelhampton on your own, as I have done, and not in a coach party.

The interior is memorable. In the Great Hall—the chief feature of all these medieval dwellings, there is exceptionally fine linenfold panelling; look up, and there is a timbered ceiling that was designed and constructed five hundred years ago, and with such skilled craftsmanship

134

Athelhampton House

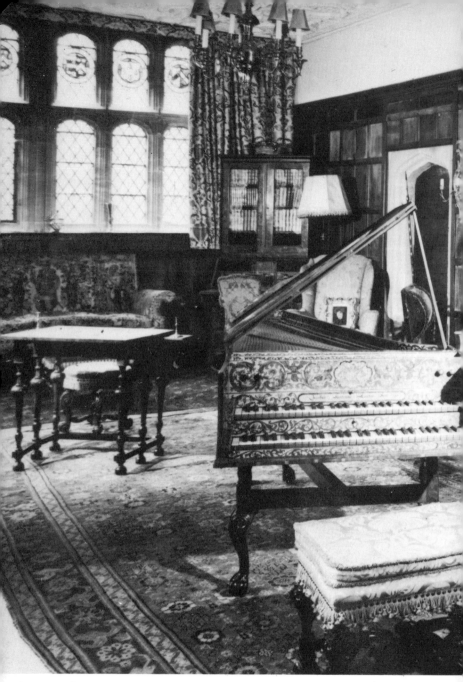

Great Chamber, Athelhampton House

King's Room, Athelhampton House

that it has hardly required attention since the joiners laid down their tools. It is matched by another timber ceiling, and more panelling, in the King's Ante-Room, which is connected by way of an unmistakable Tudor arch to the Great Chamber, or Drawing-Room, beyond.

All about you, in every room, there is furniture—not screened off, as all too often, but looking as though it was in everyday use by the family until quite recently. Portraits and tapestries on the walls, of course; an unusual feature and, you may feel, something of an anachronism among so much splendid oak, an 18th-century harpsichord that once belonged to Queen Charlotte herself. There is the State Bedroom, the term implying noble, and possibly royal use; there is the Long Gallery; there are secret rooms, as so often in Great Houses whose owners have at one time or another had to shelter refugees from political or religious persecution; there are staircases—features which are so often show-pieces, whether of polished oak or the more spectacular stone ones to be seen in the larger of our Great Houses, which may prefer the alternative title, Stately Homes.

Take your time at Athelhampton, for there is so much to see. The house stands amid many acres of gardens, some of which were laid out anew less than a hundred years ago by one Inigo Thomas, who favoured the style generally known as 'Italian' and was encouraged by its then owners to design and build walls and a 'corona', making use of Ham Hill stone in particular. As, reluctantly, you walk away, glance back over your shoulder and consider again the beauty, the symmetry and the proportions of the oriel windows that grace and lighten the L-shaped façade. In sheer size, this cannot compare with that of Forde Abbey; but for one lover of Dorset anyway it ranks as the most perfect gem of them all.

If there is beauty in the stonework of the county's buildings, whether large or small, public or private, old or new, there is beauty also in her many bridges. The relatively few rivers—Stour, Piddle, Frome, Lydden, Tarrant, Brit and Cerne are the best known—tend to run leisurely, as befits the tempo generally prevailing; for the most part they run through wide valleys, bordered by extensive water-meadows; the bridges that span them therefore tend to be impressively long and multi-arched. There are a considerable number of them, and they are all well worth seeking out and examining closely. You can rarely do this properly from the road which they carry from one bank to the other; but you can do so by leaving them at either end to look at them as they deserve to be looked at, either from upstream or downstream according to the

Sturminster Newton Bridge

position of the sun at the time. The upstream side is usually the better, as it will have cutwaters which may not have been built on the downstream side. All are highly photogenic, in addition to being outstanding artefacts in their own right on a major scale; the variously shaped arches, curved or pointed, and the sharp or angular edges of the piers and cutwaters, offer strong contrasts in light and shadow, and black-and-white photographs of them are usually more rewarding than any taken in colour, for obvious reasons.

Just south of Sturminster Newton there is a very fine example of one such bridge. It was built some time around the year 1500 and consists of six pointed arches, with chiselled cornices and moulded coping-stones. The Stour flows gently through the arches, easing its way past the cutwaters and spreading again to wash the banks of the water-meadows on either side. Sunlight and alternating shadow beneath cornice and arch give the façade of the bridge an added dimension. When you return to the road from the river bank, look along the line of either parapet, and you will appreciate even more fully the skill of those medieval stonemasons who designed and made the gentle curve upwards and then downwards from one end of the long bridge to the other; it is so slight as to seem, from water level, to be almost a straight line.

Set in the stonework of one of the cutwaters just short of the Blandford-bound road is one of the many iron plaques that are still to be seen on these bridges of Dorset.

Warning Plaque on Sturminster Newton Bridge

Wool Bridge

The plaque was not addressed to vandals (as might be the case today, even if less menacingly worded) but as a warning to carriers. In this case the ancient bridge was the means of access from the old road to the 17th-century watermill just upstream to which corn in bulk was carted at harvest-time in huge loads on broad-tyred wagons and from which the ground flour was subsequently carried back across the bridge to the customers. As wagons grew larger and heavier there was an ever-increasing threat to the stability of bridges such as these, built in medieval times before such weights were anticipated; they were a vital necessity of communication, and their preservation was a matter of urgency. You will find this plaque, of cast iron, the lettering set off against white paint, on most if not all of Dorset's major bridges.

It appears on Wool Bridge, spanning the Frome near the village of that name, five miles to the west of Wareham. Again, it is multi-arched, but in this case the arches are rounded. Immediately above and overlooking it from the north bank is one of Dorset's lesser manor houses, Woolbridge Manor. Bridge and manor house both date from the Elizabethan period, though the date is not known exactly. Of the two, perhaps it is the manor house that chiefly strikes the eye. Its main fabric is composed of a pleasant mingling of stonework and brickwork, both of them mellow. Because of the presence of some ugly outbuildings, the beauty of the manor house can only be appreciated from certain positions but the trio of tall chimney-stacks, ornamental and distinct from one another, soar towards the sky, each upon an individ-

ual gable-end. A good deal of restoration became necessary in the late seventeenth century as the manor house itself was damaged during the Civil War.

The setting is beautiful, with the wide Frome flowing silently by almost at its feet, with swans afloat upon its surface or perched on one or other of the islets that interrupt its course not far from the bridge. Trees overhang the river bank. And the Hardy enthusiast will be particularly interested in Woolbridge Manor because it was formerly the home of the Turbervilles, and the author of the Wessex novels made use of it as the setting for the tragic honeymoon of the central figure in *Tess of the D'Urbervilles*. The bridge and the adjacent manor house are half a mile to the north of the actual village of Wool and several hundred yards from the railway crossing and sidings. You can obtain a good long-shot view of them both if you stand with your back to the crossing, with the water-meadows and river immediately in front of you and the tree-clad slopes of Wool Hill receding towards the skyline and forming a kindly backdrop to the main feature of the landscape.

Ten miles or so to the north and back in the valley of the Stour again, you will come to the village of Spettisbury, on the main road to Bland-ford Forum. The village is less picturesque than most hereabouts, chiefly because it is more or less strung out along the main road. Just short of it, to the south, there is its small church, perhaps most eye-catch-ing because, unusually, there is a pair of stocks close by the south porch. Beyond, there are some enchanting examples of ornamental-thatched cottages. And by 'ornamental' I do not simply mean that the thatch has been skilfully shaped over the dormers and eaves and round the chim-neys; there is more to it than this.

You will see on many of the thatched buildings of Dorset, perhaps more in this area then elsewhere, what might not unreasonably be termed the thatcher's 'signature'. Not content with having made a crafts-manlike job of laying thatch for a roof, he has given it his own 'mark' by designing and constructing some creature, usually a bird, and placing

Spettisbury Church and Stocks

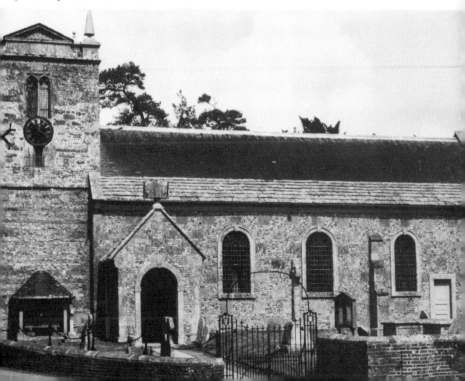

Ornamented Thatch, Spettisbury

this at one end of the ridge; or placing one at each end of the ridge, over the gable-ends; or placing a pair of such birds part way along the ridge, near enough to speak to one another, almost beak to beak. Usually they are pheasants, though they may be something as exotic as a peacock, in which case craftsmanship has stepped into the realm of true artistry. Occasionally they are not birds at all but some creature such as weasel or stoat or squirrel; and they may be placed in position not just on the line of the ridge but on the fair face of the thatch as it spreads downwards to the eaves—of course on the side where they may most easily be seen. There was, and may be still, a family of thatchers with a long tradition handed down from father to son; it was based in the village of Iwerne Courtney, a good deal farther up the valley, but their reputation spread in all directions and their work has for long been in demand.

On your left-hand side as you enter Spettisbury, there is a narrow road slanting steeply upwards from the main road. If you follow it, it will lead you to one of the county's less-well-known Iron Age hill-top forts, or camps—a subject we shall be turning to in the closing pages of this chapter. It is known alternatively as Crawford Castle and Spettis-

144

Crawford Bridge, Spettisbury

bury Rings; no 'castle', as such, of course, but turf ramparts such as are to be seen elsewhere on a larger, more dramatic scale.

This narrow road is a continuation of the road from the village of Tarrant Crawford, half a mile or so across the water-meadows to the east, that climbs briefly but steeply up from the bridge across the Stour at this point. The bridge is one of the finest, and oldest, in the county. It is odd that it should be named after the village the road left behind it a mile and more distant, rather than the village that lies a bare hundred yards beyond it; nevertheless, Crawford Bridge it is, and always has been. It is a handsome bridge, with no fewer than nine arches. It was originally built as long ago as 1235, or thereabouts, though work has been done on it since, widening and strengthening it. There are no records of any watermill anywhere in the region, so perhaps traffic has never been heavy upon it, and that may account for the remarkable condition in which it is to be seen today, after more than seven centuries of useful life.

Bridges, of whatever type or size or period, are always attractive and photogenic features of the landscape. The tally of major bridges in Dorset can very easily be extended. There is Grey's Bridge, at the foot of Dorchester's High Street, which has already been mentioned. But there are the smaller bridges, too. There is, for instance, the arched packhorse bridge at an angle of the narrow lane that leads to Fifehead Neville. You come upon it unexpectedly, set against a thick hedge and curving alongside a shallow ford that can be almost completely dry in

145

Packhorse Bridge, Fifehead Neville

summer but become impassable during and after periods of heavy rain. The bridge crosses the stripling Divelish, a tributary of the Stour. It is always a pleasure to come across these small bridges, whether, as in this case, they have simple white-painted rails and posts or more solidly built stone ramparts; they are reminders of the days when men went on foot, or on horseback, or led pack-trains of ponies cross-country in all weathers, linking one small isolated community with another, the bringers of news both good and ill, unhurried, self-sufficient, reliable.

There are other interesting and often impressive examples of the use of stone, besides the Great Houses and the multi-arched bridges. They may be on a much smaller scale, but nevertheless they are as often well worth looking at. One such is on the outskirts of the old market town of Stalbridge, some five miles to the north of Fifehead Neville's packhorse bridge. It is a market cross shaft, curiously remote from the township itself and, unlike most of its fellows in medieval market towns throughout the country, never enclosed or even roofed. It stands on a plinth of stone to a height of perhaps fifteen feet or more, silhouetted against a backdrop of foliage overhanging a stone wall.

The stonework is mellow, and softer than that of the bridges, and so has weathered more than these have done. Since it is at least six hundred years old it is perhaps not surprising that it has been so affected even by the gentle air of Dorset. When first erected, it was elaborately carved with figures and other motifs. These are now blurred and indistinct, in strong contrast with the elaborate and intricate crucifixion

146

Medieval Cross, Stalbridge

Brace of Pheasants, Plush

scene which is of much more recent date and carved in a paler and, one hopes, more weather-resistant stone, as the uppermost stage of the shaft, some three feet of it or so, tapering to a delicately sculptured finial.

The inns of Dorset are, as one would expect, a delight, each with its own character. *The Wise Man* at West Stafford, Hardy's Talbothays, a hamlet some three miles to the east of Dorchester, brings us back to the subject of thatch; it has as entertaining an ornamental thatched roof as any in the county. The roof itself is beautifully moulded, not only round the base of the chimney-stacks and over the gable-ends but over the small semi-circular porch. It is even more remarkable, however, for the distribution of an assortment of creatures perched not only on the ridge-pole but down the long slope towards the eaves. They are, all of them, quite disconcertingly lifelike, both in their fashioning and in their stance. Two of them are manifestly, and even from a distance, cock-pheasants; another is curiously reminiscent of Brian-the-Snail in the television series, Magic Roundabout. They may well be the 'signatures' of that family of expert thatchers who have lived so long in Iwerne Courtney, nearly twenty miles away to the north-west.

Whole chapters, even a book of modest length, could be written about the Dorset inn. There is *Stocks Inn,* for example, in the village of Holt, to the north of Wimborne, with its set of village stocks beside the door. There is the *St Peter's Finger* at Lytchett Minster, to the south of Wimborne, with its beautifully painted sign of the most unusual name,

Wise Man Inn, West Stafford

St Peter *ad Vincula* (the corruption here is simply explained). There is the stone-built *Greyhound Inn* (now unhappily announcing itself as 'Hotel'), crouching long and low beneath the gaunt ruins of Corfe Castle, focal point of the Isle of Purbeck, with its squat pillared porch supporting a small room. There is the *Elm Tree*, at Langton Herring, with its smugglers' bolt-hole beneath the stone-slab floor, and the oak beam overhead, from a hook in which the victim of an old-time 'kangaroo court' was hanged by the neck till he was dead.

The temptation to continue is hard to resist! Back in Plush there is the charming *Brace of Pheasants*. Cob walls and thatched roof, five small, high-set windows, this was once a small row of cottages, with a smithy at the right-hand end. Its most distinctive feature, however, is its sign: two pheasants, cock and hen, most realistically perched on a small branch, facing one another, the whole enclosed in a glass case such as you would more often see over the mantelpiece of the bar of an inn in trout-fishing country. Far to the south-west, at Whitchurch Canonicorum, there is the *Shave Cross*, the name, like its better-known fellow at Shipton-under-Wychwood in the Cotswolds, *The Shaven Crown*, indicative of monastic associations.

And so, finally ('What,' you will ask, 'will the line stretch out to the crack of doom?'), to the allegedly smallest inn in England, at Godmanstone in the valley of the Cerne. The *Smith's Arms* makes this claim. Its vital statistics are nineteen feet by eleven feet. By my reckoning, this amounts to a fraction over 200 square feet in all. The landlord agrees. What I did not like to tell him when I last called in there—for he is half a head and several stone more than I am in height and weight—is that the *Guinness Book of Records* gives *The Nutshell*, in Bury St Edmunds, as fifteen feet ten inches by seven feet six inches. That measures up to about 120 square feet. I do not know that particular inn, or landlord; but I would dearly like to see the two landlords meet and have the matter out; it could be a heroic duel! The *Smith's Arms* allegedly became an inn because Charles II stopped at the smithy, as it then was, and called for a glass of ale. The smith could not oblige. Instead of being penalised, he was promptly given a licence, and from that day onwards it has been ale rather than horseshoe nails, which had been the monarch's main problem three hundred years ago. But the landlord of *The Nutshell* certainly has the edge over his rival so far as the name is concerned; unique, I think, in the country, whereas *Smith's Arms* are ten-a-penny.

The stone-built structures, be they abbeys or manor houses, medieval crosses, Roman walls, market cross shafts or ruined castles, stand proud from the soil that bears them, over the underlying stone from which they were built. So too do the innumerable half-timbered, cob-walled and thatched lesser buildings, the farmsteads and cottages and inns scattered about the fair face of Dorset. But Dorset was peopled many centuries, even thousands of years, before even the earliest of these buildings, the walls the Romans built at Durnovaria, came into existence.

It is almost certain that this county was the first to become the home of the nomadic-type folk who had made their way across the English Channel from the continent of Europe during the Neolithic Age and earlier—several thousands of years before the coming of the Romans, and even before the Iron Age. Though no exact dates can be substantiated, there were Neolithic, Megalithic and Bronze Age men here who settled down and established themselves in the chalk uplands, the Dor-

Smiths Arms, Godmanstone

set Downs. Evidence of their existence, of their increasingly settled way of life, is to be found beneath, rather than above, the turf over which we tramp today.

This skin of turf is thin. Indeed, it is from the artificial contours it presents, more even than from the artefacts discovered when excavators are at work, that we derived our first suspicions of this age-old occupation of what came to be known, some thousands of years later, as the Kingdom of Wessex. The kingdom embraced more than just Dorset, it is true: parts of Wiltshire and Hampshire and Somerset were originally included, and Thomas Hardy took this into account when writing his Wessex novels. Wessex was so named when the West Saxons moved into the territory from the beach-heads a hundred miles and more to the east.

The evidence lies almost entirely in sites which will be marked variously on your maps as 'Camp', or 'Castle', or 'Rings', and very likely in Gothic print. Almost invariably they are to be found on the tops of rounded hills, or distributed along whaleback ridges. The highest-sited of them all is on Pilsdon Pen, 909 feet above sea level, though the one on Eggardon Hill comes to within a hundred feet of that. There are others, of varying altitude, size and shape: Dogberry Gate Camp, Lambert's Castle, Wears Hill Camp, Higher Coombe Camp, Badbury Rings, Coney's Castle, Hod Hill, Knowlton Rings, Rawlsbury Camp, and so on. These are just a few of them; your larger-scale walker's map will show many more, and will draw your attention, too, to the countless prehistoric burial-mounds such as the Long Barrows at Pimperne and Long

151

Bredy. There are more than forty of these in Dorset. Taken with the hill-top forts, camps, rings or castles, they offer more evidence of the existence of prehistoric man in Dorset than anywhere else in England; nor is Wiltshire, with Avebury and Stonehenge, being deliberately ignored in this context.

How, though, to *see* these important and often very striking records of men who came to these shores five thousand years ago and were followed by successive waves of like-minded immigrants until well on into the Iron Age, where they were first encountered by the Romans at the turn of the century from B.C. to A.D.? You must drive or, where as is so often necessary, foot-slog your way from valley to valley by way of the summits in between to see for yourself what is marked for you on your map. Even if the site is marked as 'Castle', it will not be what this word naturally leads you to expect. No stonework here, as at Corfe and elsewhere. These hill-top sites consist of turfed-over earth embankments of greater or lesser extent, rectangular with well-rounded corners, elliptical or round or lop-sided according to the contours of the hill top on which they were constructed. Time, measured in thousands of years, has softened the outlines of the ramparts as originally laid out, worn away the raised sections, filled-in the ditches between them, obliterated the holes in which, if any, posts had been set as additional protection; time, wind and weather have done their best to restore the contours to their original form. Save for the very outstanding examples, such as Eggardon, it takes a practised eye very often to establish the existence of many of these hill-top sites, their lay-out, size and proportions that may have been indicated on an archaeological map.

Ideally, they should be seen from the air, but not everyone can afford to hire a helicopter, or even a hot-air balloon. The alternative—and it can be a frustrating one—is to time your visit so that the sun is low to the east or west, when even the faintest of near-obliterated turf embankments may cast a slight shadow, distinguishing the man-made from the natural.

Unlike the abbeys and manor houses, bridges and inns, these hill-top sites cannot claim to be photogenic (from ground level); it is rarely worth your while to carry a camera up to these summits, often on quite steep and challenging slopes, unless the day is unusually clear and you want a long-distance shot from, rather than to, the site in question. But such long-distance shots, especially with telephoto lenses, can be rewarding; and they are a reminder that the sites themselves were specifically selected by prehistoric man, not only because they were clear of the trees that filled so much of the valleys and the lower-lying ground but because they afforded him the chance to keep watch on the potential marauding enemy, who might approach from any quarter of the compass.

Hambledon Hill, half a mile to the south of Iwerne Courtney (or Shroton, on some maps), and Hod Hill, two miles to the south, though they do not begin to compare in height with Eggardon, are among the finest examples of these hill-top sites; indeed, the first-named is the largest and most impressive of the score and more of such sites, always excepting Maiden Castle, to which we shall come very shortly. Both are situated on high ground rising steeply from the valleys of the Stour and one of its tributaries. The bastion-like ramparts of Hambledon Camp offer a hint of what is to be seen, on an altogether vaster scale twenty miles or so to the south-west at Maiden Castle. Both are essentially Iron Age sites, though Hambledon could quite easily have been constructed during an earlier period and elaborated when Iron Age man took possession of it two or three thousand years ago. It is superbly sited, with immense views in every direction from an altitude of well over 600 feet.

All the same, these are no more than 'starters' to the feast, the grandest, noblest and most impressive of all these reminders of prehistoric man's presence in Dorset, Maiden Castle, a couple of miles to the south-west of Dorchester and easily approached by one or more minor roads. There is nothing comparable with this earthwork; it is the largest, not merely in the county, not merely in England, but in all Europe. It is also by far the most elaborately designed.

It is more than half a mile long and almost a quarter of a mile wide. It consists of a flattish, kidney-shaped area of some 130 acres of turf land enclosed within a system of double, and sometimes triple ramparts with continuous V-shaped ditches between them and a highly complex arrangement of alternating bastion walls and deep ditches to defend the main entrances. The ramparts still rise to a height of some ninety feet even after the passing of four or perhaps five thousand years, though the once V-shaped ditches are now U-shaped with the washing down of earth and stone during these millennia. Unlike the hill-top forts, Maiden Castle is relatively low-lying; it stands some 600 feet above sea level, but the surrounding terrain is pastureland, only very gently undulating. You might describe Maiden Castle, as seen from the air, as kidney-shaped.

Possibly, as well as being by far the largest, it is also the first to have been designed, laid out and occupied by Celtic invaders from the Continent of Europe, and there is no question that successive communities occupying it enlarged and strengthened the site first established by their fore-runners. The first of these were probably from Brittany, but the site that you see today was already in the form that was known to Iron

Maiden Castle

Age man, who adapted it in certain specific ways to his own use. It has been more thoroughly excavated and analysed—by Sir Mortimer Wheeler, among others before and since—than any other site of the kind in the whole country. There are massive stakes in the ramparts, and within these great retaining walls there were wooden huts; not only men and their families but small herds of cattle and flocks of sheep, and even dogs, were occupants of this vast site; animal bones have been found there and identified without difficulty.

Long before the Romans had worked their way westwards into Dorset, round about the year 43 A.D., the Britons were well established here, and in control of the region. Also, though they were not in fact looking for trouble, they were prepared for it if it did come. And of course it did come; the Romans knew what they were about.

There is plenty of evidence of the Briton's preparedness. When the Romans set about besieging and ultimately storming these formidable ramparts, topped then by massive timber palisades, they had a well-equipped body of men to contend with. The Britons, of course, were in the end no match for the well-disciplined and ably commanded legionaries, and their ages-old settlement was doomed to fall. Their sling-stones made relatively little impression on the shields and the famous *testitudo* of the Roman soldiery. Vast numbers of men died during the siege and eventual conquest of Maiden Castle, Romans and Britons alike. Not so many years ago, a mass grave was located and opened up. It contained skeletons too numerous to count; nor was it possible to decide which were those of the Britons and which those of the Romans. Many of them still had axe-heads embedded in their skulls or between their ribs—evidence that these were the attackers rather than the defenders. Near the communal grave there was discovered an 'ammunition-pit' which proved to contain no fewer than 20,000 sling-stones; the remainder had no doubt rattled against the Roman shields and, in many cases, cracked the legionaries' skulls. There is little doubt that they were selected stones from among the smaller pebbles of Chesil Bank. I have used one of these as a paperweight for many, many years.

When the Romans had finally ousted the occupants of Maiden Castle they took little further interest in the site; instead, they turned their attention to a more promising site that was to become their Durnovaria, now Dorchester, Hardy's Casterbridge. Maumbury Rings, immediately to the south of the town they built, a matter of only a few hundred yards, are not, as you might suspect from the name, the relic of a hill fort but in fact the remains of an amphitheatre, built, as always, close to any Roman town for the entertainment of the soldiery and the

155

civilians who moved in once the stronghold was established. Pound-bury Camp, on the diametrically opposite side of the town, was a Roman site, not a prehistoric one: a reminder, today, that the map must be read with care, and not too much taken for granted.

Yet Maiden Castle was not completely abandoned by the Romans after they had overrun it and wiped out the community that had lived within its ramparts, and stolen their sheep and cattle. Comparatively recent excavations there have revealed, near the eastern entrance, the foundations and other remains of what must have been a Romano-British temple that dated from some time in the third or fourth century A.D. Here, though we do not know exactly what form it took, there was the worship of some pagan god—Mithras, perhaps; in spite of official opposition, he was worshipped by many of the legionaries manning Hadrian's Wall, three hundred and more miles to the north.

This is perhaps as good a point at which to say farewell to Dorset; at any rate for me. For it was at Maiden Castle, indeed within the turf-clad ramparts, that I experienced, some forty years ago, my closest and most truly unforgettable contact with what I must call the *genius loci* that pervades this whole county.

I had turned off the main Dorchester-Bridport road and taken the then narrow lane that leads to within a hundred yards or so of the hill fort. I wheeled my bicycle over the sloping turf until I came to the maze of ramparts and ditches that interlock to form the complex entrance to the spacious interior. I came to a newly excavated pit, in which the 20,000 sling-stones lay. Close by was a newly opened grave, with the bleached skulls and bones of two distinct skeletons lying, knees bent to their chins, on the earth-and-chalk floor. Within a few yards of these, I pitched my one-man bivouac tent.

I had already had a meal in Dorchester, so I undressed and slid into my sleeping-bag. But sleep was slow to come, though I was tired from a long day in the saddle. Alone within those vast ramparts, with only a quarter-moon in the sky to enable me to appreciate the darkness all about me, I found myself envisaging, with ever-increasing intensity, the activities, spread over so many generations, so many hundreds of years, that had brought about the creation of this vast site. Prehistoric man possessed no implements save antler-picks and, for spades, at best the shoulder-blades of oxen. With such implements, and perhaps the use of crudely woven baskets, they had dug and carried the chalky soil beneath this thin, grey-green turf that is unchanged to this day, hollowed out the great ditches and built the ramparts above them.

What spirit—over and above the desire for security for themselves and their belongings—had animated them, so that they laboured for so long to achieve so stupendous a monument to their day and age? Had it something in common with that which animated the builders of Avebury and Stonehenge in neighbouring Wiltshire? Did they have a unifying religion, interpreted by some early priesthood? There *must* have been some all-powerful influence that inspired and co-ordinated their activites, the very lives of these, the earliest settlers in Dorset, and those who came after them.

What this was, what form it took, we shall in all probability never now discover. But for all its mellow beauty, its intimacy, its variety, Dorset happily remains a region of England fraught with mystery; it holds its secrets still, and well. For my own part, I accept this gladly. I realised it for the first time that night I spent alone in a small tent at Maiden Castle; I have never lingered in, or even passed through, that beloved county without being made aware yet once again of the *genius loci* whose presence I so strongly, unforgettably, felt that night so long ago.

Index

BRISTO

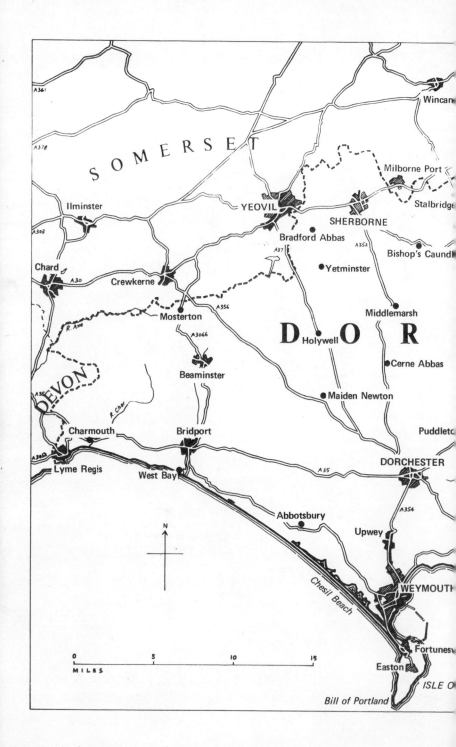